SET

THE FURY
OF EGYPT

SET
THE FURY OF EGYPT

*Edited and compiled
by Asenath Mason & Bill Duvendack*

Temple of Ascending Flame

2019

LIST OF CONTENTS

LORD OF STORM AND CHANGE

Asenath Mason

In the last few decades the interest in Set, one of ancient Egypt's earliest gods, has been given much attention by occult communities, magical orders and solitary practitioners interested in the Left Hand Path. As a self-created god, Set is an archetype of the Adversary and an attractive model for a practitioner seeking initiation into mysteries of self-deification. Feared by the faint-hearted and worshipped by those who sought power, he became a symbol of storm and change, movement and transformation, force and energy. His fiery nature represents lust and fury, which is the driving force on the path, and his Black Flame is the inner spark of Godhood that successively becomes the fiery pillar of ascent on the path of self-initiation. His forked knife cuts attachments to the surrounding world, liberating the initiate from bonds of slavery and mindless ignorance, and his scepter represents authority and power over destiny.

These portrayals of Set and many more are the subject of the book you are now holding in your hands. We will look here into his origins, ancient myths and legends, and modern interpretations of his role on the Left Hand Path. It is not possible to examine them all in a single tome, though, and that is not the purpose of this book. The idea behind this anthology is to provide insights into the nature and role of Set from the perspective of the Draconian Tradition and as such he is approached in essays and rituals presented here.

For the start, however, let us focus on the definitions. Like other deities associated with darkness and chaos, Set has many aspects and many faces and his character is highly ambivalent. He is the son of the earth god Geb and Nut, the goddess of the sky, and the brother of Osiris, Isis, and Nephthys, who is also believed to be his wife and consort. This is how Set is presented in the Osiris myth, which is a prominent theme in ancient Egyptian mythology. In the Pyramid Texts, however, he is described as the son of Ra himself and the brother of Horus the Elder. The Greek version of his name is Seth, while other variations include Setech, Setekh, Setesh, Sutuach, and Sutekh. The etymology and the meaning of the name are not entirely clear, though. It is usually translated as "isolator" or "he who separates." It may also be derived from two Egyptian words, i.e. "setes," meaning "pillar," or "seten" – "to blind." In the sources dating to the first centuries CE (known as the Greek Magical Papyri or PGM) we also find "magical" names of Set used in invocations and spells: Erbeth, Pakerbeth, and Bolchoseth. Their meaning is not known, either, but they appear all over enchantments from the Hermetic period and possibly signify the nature of Set blended with the deities from the contemporary Greek lore.

The most known story of Set is the myth about the conflict with his brother Osiris in which Set is portrayed as the usurper and the enemy of the "king of the living." According to the story, Osiris and his sister and wife Isis ruled Egypt, creating laws and teaching their followers the secrets of agriculture, crafts and medicine. Their power over the land, however, made Set jealous, and once when they went for a journey to visit their worshippers, he and seventy two accomplices prepared a plan to murder Osiris. They made a special coffer designed to fit Osiris and during a great feast, supposedly in his honor, Set tricked his brother to lay down in it. He said that whoever could fit in the chest, which was beautiful and richly ornamented, would win it. Once Osiris was in the chest, Set's accomplices nailed down the lid and threw it into the Nile. This happened on the seventeenth day of the month Hathor. After a long search, Isis found the coffer and hid it with the intention of giving her husband a proper burial. Set, however, found the chest and tore it open. Then he cut up his brother's corpse, throwing the parts of his body all over the land of Egypt. Thus, again, Isis went for a search, this time accompanied by her sister Nephthys, who left Set to help with the quest to restore Osiris. Eventually, they managed to find all body parts except for the phallus, which was eaten by a fish. This was not the end of Set's struggle for the rule over Egypt, though. After his brother's death he had to fight Osiris' son Horus in the war that took eighty years and ended with Horus' victory, even though he lost his eye in the fight. After the war Set was forced to return it to Horus, who then became the Lord of the Two Lands.

In ancient Egyptian myths, Set and Osiris (or Horus) represent two conflicting and yet complementary forces in the universe: light and darkness. As the lord of the barren desert, Set is the opposing principle to Osiris, who is the god of fertility and agriculture. As he who slays his brother, he became the embodiment of all that is evil, dark and chaotic in the world, and the Greeks identified him with Typhon, the terrifying monster representing all death and destruction. While Osiris stood for the life-giving Nile, Set was the god of the desert that took life away. For this reason he was often associated with monsters and beasts threatening the world order such as Apep, the serpent of chaos who tried to devour the sun god Ra every day on his nightly passage through the underworld. Set has a chthonic aspect as well - his breath makes vermin crawl out from the ground. As the lord of the chthonic regions, he is thought to devour the souls of those who travel to the underworld. He is also a god of metals created within the bowels of the earth, especially iron, which was believed to be "the bones of Set" and thought to be the hardest of metals and the symbol of strength. In the writings of the Greek scholar Plutarch from the first century CE we read:

> "Typhon, as has been said, is named Seth and Bebon and Smu, and these names would indicate some forcible and preventive check or opposition or reversal. Moreover, they call the loadstone the bone of Horus, and iron the bone of Typhon, as Manetho records. For, as the iron oftentimes acts as if it were being attracted and drawn toward the stone, and oftentimes is rejected and repelled in the opposite direction, in the same way the salutary and good and rational movement of the world at one time, by persuasion, attracts and draws toward itself and renders more gentle that harsh and Typhonian movement, and then again it gathers itself together and reverses it and plunges it into difficulties."

In this sense, Set and Osiris/Horus typify the universal polarity within the world that is the foundation of all harmony and dynamics of all its processes. Set is the lord of darkness, the enemy of the sun, the master of chaos, and the god of war. He is responsible for earthquakes, storms and eclipses - all phenomena that were believed to pose a threat to the natural order of the universe. When Egypt was invaded by foreign armies (especially the Assyrians), Set became the god of outlanders and all hostile forces existing outside the land. His domain is the night, the thunder, the storm, the scorching sun of the desert, and in the Book of the Dead he is called the Lord of the Northern Sky. He is also the red god, red being the color of the desert sands, bloodshed in battle, or fire destroying everything.

However, Set was not always viewed as the embodiment of all that is evil and chaotic. One of his titles was "the mighty one" or "he of great strength" and in Upper Egypt he was sometimes believed to be the equivalent of the god-king Horus of Lower Egypt. This was Horus the Elder, the god of the sky during daytime, while Set was viewed as the god of the night sky. In art from the Old and Middle Kingdoms we encounter depictions of these two gods together representing the union of Upper and Lower Egypt, and the union of these two gods was Horus-Set, a man with two heads, of which one was that of the hawk and the other of the Set animal. At the time of the Hyksos Dynasty ("rulers of foreign land") Set was the leading deity, and he was also the chief god in the Ramesside Period, during the reign of the XIX and XX Dynasties. The name Sethos or Seti, characteristic for the kings from this period, is derived from his name. Set is also the deity that kills the serpent Apophis (Apep). There are depictions of the solar barque that show Set defending the Sun God Ra, fighting the serpent, and the barque is pulled not by jackals but the animals of Set. People in Kharga Oasis worshipped Set as their god, portraying him as a falcon fighting Apophis. His relationship with the serpent of chaos is not clearly defined in the myths, though, as he alternately appears as he who kills the monster and he who controls him, and sometimes Set and Apep are identified with each other. Set was also the patron deity of the dead and he was sometimes depicted helping Osiris ascend to heaven.

Animals associated with Set included e.g. the antelope, the donkey, the pig, the hippopotamus, and the crocodile. Set himself was worshipped under the guise of a mysterious animal resembling a dog, jackal or fennec fox. The characteristic features of the animal were long rectangular ears, a curved snout, a thin forked tail and canine body with fur tufts in the shape of an inverted arrow. In many depictions he is also presented as a human with the head of his animal.

The cult of Set probably originated in the XI Nome of Upper Egypt, where the Set animal was a characteristic symbol. His major cult center, however, was in Ombos, a town on the west bank of the river Nile. There were also other sanctuaries dedicated to Set, such as Oxyrhynchus in upper Egypt, for instance.

In the Greco-Roman period he became a deity associated with magic, especially the magic of war and destruction. He was called to protect caravans traveling through the desert as well as to create sandstorms and destroy enemies. His domain was the northern part of the sky and his dwelling place was the Great Bear constellation. The north in many cultures was believed to be the place of death, darkness and cold - principles commonly associated with Set. People feared that Set can interrupt celebrations dedicated to other deities and to appease his anger they sacrificed animals connected with his cult. Plutarch writes that before each full moon in the month of Pachons an antelope was killed as an offering to Set. At the time of the winter solstice in the month of Choiak he was given a donkey. And in the first day of the month Mesore, at the feast of Heru Behutet, people sacrificed birds and fish to Set. His opposing force was the goddess Reret, who was depicted as a hippopotamus, and whose main role was to protect people of Egypt from the evil influence of the Lord of Darkness. However, the same goddess, known also as Taweret or Taurt, was also believed to be his wife and it was also thought that she kept him chained within the seven stars of the Great Bear constellation, which were her domain as well. The main festival of Set was his birthday, which in the modern calendar falls on the sixteenth day of July. Other days associated with the god were 18th December (third day of the month Mechir) and 2nd March (seventeenth day of the month Parmutit), known as the days when "Set comes forth."

In modern times, Set is the initiator of the Black Flame and one of the patron deities of the Left Hand Path. His title "he who isolates" refers in Setian mysteries to the concept of isolated and awakened consciousness, and the Black Flame can be viewed as a symbol of the inner center, the source of individuality, personal power and evolutionary potential of man. As he who defeats Osiris, Set represents the destruction of stasis. As the slayer of Apep, he is the symbol of victory over aimless chaos and mindless ignorance. Osiris in Setian mysteries stands for stasis, death and stagnation. His destruction is the triumph over the old world order, overcoming structures and laws that are imposed upon the individual, annihilation of the programmed patterns of thinking. This is the antinomian path of going against all that is unnatural and imposed and thus limiting the inherent potential within each human being. The killing of Apep in this interpretation is the destruction of blindness and ignorance for the sake of being the master of one's own destiny, recreation of oneself according to one's will. This is expressed through another title of Set, "Set-Heh," meaning "Eternal Set," showing his role in the process of self-initiation and individual transcendence.

In the Typhonian Tradition, Set is sometimes identified with Typhon, the serpent-dragon of chaos. According to certain theories, however, Typhon is much more than that. Gerald Massey, for instance, claimed that Typhon was a feminine force, personification of primordial darkness that preceded light and the act of creation. In one of his essays he writes:

„The first form of the Devil was female, called the Dragon of Darkness, who was Tiamat in Akkad, and Typhon in Egypt. Typhon gave birth to Sut, who became the Egyptian devil - our Satan - and who was represented by the Black jackal, the voice of Darkness; and Sut, the black one, gives us the name of Soot, the black thing."

For this reason, animals associated with Set are not only those mentioned above but also the Serpent and the Dragon of Seven Heads representing the seven stars in the Great Bear constellation. One of Set's manifestations on earth was Aiwass, an entity that made contact with Aleister Crowley in Egypt and whose words were written as a channeled book known as *The Book of the Law*. Set's name is also attributed to tunnels on the dark side of the Qabalistic Tree of Life, described by Kenneth Grant in his Typhonian Trilogies. The Tunnels of Set connect the whole Tree of Qliphoth, and the entrance to the labyrinth is believed to exist within the hidden Sephira Daath - Knowledge. Grant often refers to the Qabalistic Abyss as the Desert of Set, connecting it with the mythical Lord of Darkness. This concept resembles the Roba El Khaliyeh desert of Arabic lore, described as "the red desert." In ancient times it was believed that the desert was inhabited by ghouls, damned souls and evil spirits, which corresponds to the idea of the Qliphoth, which are portrayed as the dwelling places of demons and abominations. Therefore, as the initiator of the Qliphothic Path, Set represents the creative energy that is chaotic and difficult to harness but containing unlimited potential. The ability to use it for the sake of growth and expansion of consciousness is an important step in Setian mysteries of the Left Hand Path.

In this book you will find glimpses into these mysteries, provided by active practitioners of Draconian magic and initiates of the Left Hand Path. Essays and poetry, portraits and sigil art, rituals and meditations - all this contributes to the portrayal of Set as a god that is still alive and active in modern times, perhaps even more than ever before. He will enter your life like a tornado, destroying all that needs to die and clearing the way for you to build your own universe. He will teach you how to ignite the inner flame and transform it into a pillar of ascent. He will show you how to devour your gods and be the master of your destiny. And he will guide you on the path of fire and storm, showing you the way to your own Godhood. Let us then begin the journey.

FRAGMENTS AND FIGMENTS

Bill Duvendack

There's not a lot I can say about Set that has not already been discussed before, and in more in-depth pieces. Being one of the most popular but enigmatic deities of ancient Egypt, Set has captured the imagination and speculation of many thinkers from many walks of life over the years and especially since the discovery and translation of the Rosetta Stone in 1799 E.V. However, for all of this speculation, there are a few pieces that are constantly neglected when it comes to understanding him. In this brief essay I will discuss some of these more factual parts of his character so that the reader gets a more complete and comprehensive look and understanding of him. This piece is also intended to be an overview for those that may not know much about him.

What's in a Name?

Although Kenneth Grant explored this in the book *Cults of the Shadow*, there has not been a lot discussed about it otherwise. At a cursory glance we see an obvious connection:

Set, and Aset. Even the hieroglyphics of the two are connected, so we at least know that the two are connected in some way. Set is the older of the two deities, as archaeology has revealed, and while the only connection between the two comes to us from the Heliopolis ennead creation myth, we can conservatively speculate that there is much more to the story than that, and that if you look at him from a linear perspective, she would have been derived from him in some way. As many of you know, this is not part of the old stories, but truth is often times stranger than fiction.

While his name is commonly known as Set, the older version of it in hieroglyphics is *Sth*. In comparison, the name of Aset in hieroglyphs is *St*. As mentioned before, Set is the older of the two deities, and we can see that according to archaeology the two names are related, implying that there is a connection present. What this connection is, though, is unknown. Speculation tells us that she would be some sort of offspring or variant of his original character as lord of the red desert, or lord of the western desert. There is a gap of approximately 900 years between Set and Aset, and during this time were the pre-dynastic period and first four dynasties of the old kingdom. On a technical note, Aset did not come into the picture after the shift to the solar phallic pharaoh paradigm, whereas Set was present much earlier.

Keep in mind that this 900 year block of time was before his more modern correspondences having to do with chaos, evil, and all things related to those subjects. It was during this time that he was known as a god of the red desert and storms. As anyone that has spent time in the desert or understanding desert culture knows, this also means he was a nomadic god. The Bedouins of the desert are known for traveling not just for the sake of trade, but also in the name of water and food, and it is likely that Set would have embodied these traits as well. Generally, Anpu is seen as a nomadic being as well, but in the stories and myths of Egypt, he mostly haunts places of burial, so his nomadic nature is not as wide ranging as that of Set.

All of this leaves us with a few questions: 1) What is his connection to Aset? It is clear she is a derivative of him, but in what way? And why don't people work with the two of them together, since it's obvious there is ancient power there? 2) Why did some important characteristics of his nature get removed? Characteristics changing are common in deities that have existed as long as he has, but why was his nomadic nature simply removed? 3) Since Aset corresponds to the star Sirius, so too does Set. How does one incorporate working with the three of them together?

Zoomorphic Ancient Alien Experimentation Gone Wrong? Or Simply Something We Don't Know?

Let's talk about the head. His head. You know, the ant-eater. Right? Um, well, no, it's probably not an ant-eater, but you probably already knew that. As a matter of fact, no one knows what his head is, and those that claim to simply don't. This has been a topic of debate that has been going on for a long, long time, and there is no evidence or proof of what it is. Theories abound, though, from the outrageous to the logical, but there is yet to be a definitive explanation or answer to this. I am not about to claim that I have the answer either, because not only would that be presumptuous, it would also be pretentious and arrogant.

When it comes to Egyptian deities, often times we know what animal it is by looking at it, and matching what we see to the natural world around us. For example, the god Hoor, also known as Horus, has the head of a hawk, and we know hawks. Therefore, he is the hawk-headed god. In a lot of ways, this method is basic scientific method of thinking. We make an observance and try to figure out where and how it fits in with the world around us. This approach is where the idea that his head is that of an ant-eater comes from, but the good news is that the more we move into the twenty-first century, the more this answer is being dismissed for many reasons, most of them grounded in logic and science, which is the bedrock for further study. Case in point: Anpu. For centuries it has been believed that his head was that of a jackal because jackals are known to frequent cemeteries, but recent scientific evidence and discoveries have confirmed that it is in fact, the golden wolf commonly found in that part of the world, so in this way, science clarified centuries of misunderstanding, even though the misunderstanding was rooted in logic and observation. Does this scientific discovery take away from the energetic potency present of his jackal's nature? Of course not, as any competent magician knows! Rather, this new information reveals more depth to his character and reveals an esoteric layer to him to work with if we choose.

We should keep all of this in mind when contemplating the Set-Beast, as it is commonly known. There is no extant parallel creature present to our knowledge, so to find a clear and accurate solution at this time is impossible. There are a few key points that should be considered, though, when you contemplate what that head is and how to work with it. The first is that it is possible that the head of Set is a composite of several animals. Kenneth Grant touched on this fairly frequently through his Typhonian series of books, and to briefly summarize, he says that there are many beasts that correspond to Set, so why narrow it down to one exclusively? Yes, of course there is a lot more to it than that, and you will find it all laid out in his nine volume series. Thus, immediately we can see the idea of him being a composite deity that has been around for quite some time. Secondly, an ant-eater? Really? Generally and globally speaking, when a deity is corresponded to a particular creature, it is because the deity has the characteristics of said creature, and this is true with very few exceptions. When we take a closer look at Set, we see that he shares no common characteristics with the ant-eater, so logically this theory falls apart.

The next two points to consider are my personal favorites to discuss because they are a lot of fun! Channeled material has given us one of these theories, and while many may be skeptical of channeled material, it should be considered none the less. After all, almost everything is channeled in some way, shape, or form. This material has to do with Atlantean times. It has been channeled, and many believe that during Atlantean times there was experimentation on humans and animals that created animal-human hybrids, which became the foundation for many of the hybrid deities found around the world. Of course, this information cannot be verified in any way, shape, or form at this time, because the majority of what we know about Atlantis that has been confirmed comes to us from Plato, but it is possible at some point in the future more information will be discovered about this, so while we can't say this happened, we also can't say it did not. Thus, the working theory is that Set is older than ancient Egypt, coming down to us from Atlantean days, and that he was one of the earliest deities modified in this way. Plausible? Of course not, but interesting to consider? Most definitely yes. An extension of this theory injects the notion that aliens during more ancient times were responsible for this behavior in Atlantis, but here again; this is something to be looked at with skepticism. Both of these theories are great for stimulating the imagination, though, and as magicians we know that the imagination is the doorway to the astral plane and powerful works of magick.

The final point to mention, which is the most plausible and scientifically validated, is that the creature that is the head of Set is one that is now extinct. Around the time of 3800 B.C.E. there was an extinction event. It was not as major as ones that came before it, but it still occurred none the less. For example, a certain type of bovine went extinct around that time. When we're discussing things like this, we should keep in mind that there is a variance in the timeline of a few centuries, so this opens the range from 3800 B.C.E. to approximately 4000 B.C.E. This opens the door to the possibility that the creature that is the inspiration for the head of Set has now gone extinct, lost to the sands of time. Another way to process this information is to consider the fact that Set is older than what we know, and he may date back earlier than what is currently and conservatively speculated. This is true for a lot of things Egyptian, including the dating of the Sphinx, so this would not be surprising. However, this also gives us a greater antiquity when it comes to Set and the Draconian period of ancient Egypt, which existed before the rise of the earliest dynasties.

Occam's Razor should be considered with all of these theories, though, and it is wise to keep this in mind when processing all information, whether based in occultism or not. Occam's Razor is a critical thinking tool that basically states that often times the simplest explanation is usually the correct one. However, part of magick and occultism is opening our minds to all possibilities, no matter how fantastic. This is the gateway to esotericism and to further personal and spiritual development. While this does leave us with the question of what his head actually is, it also reminds us that the power ultimately rests in our hands, for it is through personal gnosis and communion with Set that we arrive at our own personal truths through unverified personal gnosis. Science and communication help us oftentimes turn this into verified personal gnosis, or shatter what we thought to be true. Shattering what we thought to be true is a characteristic of Set as anyone that has seriously worked with him knows, and it is because of this that he is one of the more intense entities to engage.

The Bringer and Protector of Light

A facet of Set that is not commonly worked with is that of his role as protector and deliverer of the light. This comes to us from the commonly known stories in which he went out in front of Ra's solar barque as it traveled through the Duat, specifically its nightly voyage through the dark and underworld. He fought the monsters of the abyss so that the Sun could rise safely the next morning, and it is in this way that he cleared the path for the Sun. This is an interesting connection because it tells us one of his most potent forms is that of combatant, but also protector and defender of the light. From a Left Hand Path perspective, this could be seen as assisting us in protecting our own inner light from threats of loss born of chaos and darkness.

This also tells us he is allied with the light, which contradicts his newer role of being the "Egyptian version of the devil," as so many people are quick to employ. As a matter of fact, we can see that this also means he is solar in a lot of ways. Aleister Crowley and many other magicians since his time have also worked with Set as an initiator of sorts, and you can see from the above story how this is true. He goes first and goes forth, opening up doors of spiritual and personal growth and creates opportunities for us to learn if we but rise to his challenges and tests. In Thelema, this is indicated and worked with through the formula Lashtal, where he is the linchpin that brings everything together. This also explains how we can work with him. Do you need some magical dirty work done? He's your guy. Are you ready to take your magick and growth to the next level? He is the one. Is it time to defend your light, or have it defended for you if you are going through intense periods of transition in your life? Again, he can easily rise to the challenge and answer the call. His alignment with the light as is illustrated by the above story is a fairly newer characteristic of his, though, but it does line up with his older correspondences of being a god of the desert. After all, other than sand and red rocks of the Egyptian desert, the Sun is the most striking element of that environment.

It should be remembered, though, that he is not necessarily an emotionally even-keel deity. This is evidenced by the fact that one of the things he governs is storms. On the one hand, this tells us he can be temperamental, but on the other it tells us he has the potency of the sky, electricity, rain, the air, and sandstorms. Many people consider him a very cold deity, but this is only partially true as the correspondence to storms tells us he is a being of intense passion, and passion is generally born out of strong emotions. He is therefore not emotionally aloof, but rather has a lot of absolute control over said emotions. Whether these emotions are born out of love for Ra or his own hidden agenda is another story, though, and one that is open to interpretation. Yes, the case could be made that he protects the light from a space of love for it. You could also make the argument he protects the light from the space of a love of conflict and battle. Ultimately, as is true with every other spirit being out there, we can never know the full story, as their ways are their own, and we are limited in our understanding due to being in physical form.

I hope this introduction to his nature and character enhances your experiences with him, and for those of you that want to know more, there are many good books out there that discuss his character in depth. These should be easy to find and broadly accessible, but like his character, you will only find what you seek if you invest in the hunt.

HYMNS
OF ADORATION
TO SETEKH

Edgar Kerval

The following working was inspired by rites of devotion to Setekh, the lord of the red desert. Such manifestations are encountered throughout the Tuat, one of the realms that are under his rule. His temple is guarded by a serpent race that is commanded through diverse incantations to let only the initiates of the Sethian mysteries enter. In the Tuat you can meet the serpent demon called "Sati-Temui," who is in charge to help devour the souls of adepts who try to cross the temple in the Tuat. Before devouring the souls, they are burned in infernal vessels of fire in the Tuat. After that, the soul is seduced by Set in the form of a giant serpent which slowly devours its essence.

For this working you will need to place an image, statue or any relevant items connected with the god. A glass of beer and Setekh incense: tobacco, red pepper, dragon's blood, or copal will be used in the working as well.

SETEKH by Kaela

Chant the different mask names provided below for several minutes until you feel the trance. Then begin the hymn and the invocation:

Nak, Sabau, Apophis, Suti, Baba, Smy, Hemhemti, Pakerbeth,
Saatet-ta, Qerneru, Tutu, Nesht, Hau-hra, Iubani, Amam,
Sebaent- Seba, Khak-ab, Khan-ru,Uai Sau, Beteshu, Kharubu

HYMN OF GLORIFICATION
(*Powers of Setekh*)

The sky turns red, the stars darken the sun,
The vaults are open, the earth trembles before his throne,
The red planet devours the souls of men,
At midnight sun Setekh rises to power,
The god who lives in his own darkness,
Who feeds on the souls through the midnight sun,
The powerful master of a cunning craft,
Whose mother knows not his name;
His glory is in hell,
His power is in the underworld;
Like a serpent dancing in the desert,
Through his voice, he is stronger than hell,
The forces of darkness are behind him,
His helpers are under his feet,
His crown on his head, his serpents on his brow,
A red serpent is on his brow,
Sutekh, devourer of souls, whose flame consumes
thousands of universes and all light on the earth.
Chants of putrefaction, power and agony,
To he who has rage and fury in his heart,
Who lives in every proclamation,
Who eats the entrails of his enemies for eternity,
Becoming the black flame that spreads his gnosis,
From the pillars of fire;
Through Amenti he has gathered his spirits,
Set has risen as the Great One, master of masters,
A mystic call for those who do not know his masks
and secret names spoken in tongues of fire.
The old kingdom rises in flames,
Devouring the ancestral fire of time.
Set, lord of the red desert, storms and darkness,
Who himself prepares the black flame.
He who feeds on the gods of the nightside,

Master of messengers of the Serpent and the Dragon!
I invoke his power, the one of the dragon at midnight!
He is the raised head of the serpent who guards the
entrance to the paths of darkness.
He is the ruler of pathways through thorns and storms.
He is the red god of the desert, slayer of lords, who cuts
their throats for pleasure,
Who rips their entrails,
Bringer of utter darkness, voice of crawling chaos.
Give us the power of the ancient wisdom!
Devourer of souls, king of the sulfurous path of Amenti!
The snake is born, his spirit is in the vessel,
The scales of the dragon reveal his many names,
Upon his brow - the Dead King's Crown;
God-Destroyer, God-Begetter,
He who was before the oldest males and females.
The Great Ones in the northern sky guard his fire,
The fire god of the Ancient Flame,
The urn burns his magnificent elixirs.
He has destroyed a thousand skies,
He has begotten the primogenial race of men
With a great power that overpowers the strength of the
mortals,
Wearing the divine mask, the great vast power burning
from his eyes,
He finds his way to devour everything.
Setekh's place is before time and space, all in one,
one in all.
Setekh is the oldest of the old,
Thousands serve him, hundreds are offered to him,
Among the living in the red desert and the sands of Amenti
for all eternity!

INVOCATION: THE AWAKENING
(The Black Sun in Amenti)

Thag'ahz Sethos Thag'ahz
Thag'ahz Sethos Thag'ahz

Elixirs from a thousand chambers,
Libations from red vessels,
The snake of fire rising through desolate gardens
of flesh and bones, pain and agony,
The red path is opened, the sacred fruit eaten,
The black sun consecrated through the
fires of transformation!

Thag'ahz Sethos Thagirion Thag'ahz
Thag'ahz Sethos Thagirion Thag'ahz

Transmuted liquid black fire, the path of brilliant darkness,
Tendrils of primal quintessence, the flesh of all desires,
Towers burning in tongues of fire, Black Sun rising in
perpetual darkness, in the Sea Of Nothingness!

Thag'ahz Sethos Thagirion Thag'ahz
Thag'ahz Sethos Thagirion Thag'ahz

Shadows emerge through black holes,
Veiled in madness and ecstasy,
Primal totems erupting with strange symbols,
And vibrating mantras of fire,
Under the stones of primogenial wisdom
below the pillars of the Black Sun in Thagirion.

Thag'ahz Sethos Thag'ahz
Thag'ahz Sethos Thag'ahz

MY JOURNEY INTO THE DESERT WITH SET

Mimi Hazim

My experience with working with Set began through my work with the temple. I began with no real expectations, and I would never have guessed the possibilities of the magickal alliance that we would form.

Much information can be read about the Egyptian god Set and his role as the god of chaos and destruction, evil murderer of Osiris, adversary of Horus. The Set that I found myself connecting with could not be limited to those simple and base qualities and titles.

What I was met with, and indeed he met me halfway, was a great teacher and initiator on the path of truth and transgression. A scapegoat of the Osirian cult. A challenger of stagnant societal and mental constructs.

I have found Set to be open and approachable within our work together. Every time I have asked for connection, he has been there to reveal new gnosis or teachings. I feel that there is a recognition between us; some understanding which, paradoxically, I have yet to consciously understand.

Whenever we meet during trance, I am shown his calling card of a great, piercing blue eye. His voice is unlike any other that I have heard in the past - an otherworldly sound of depth and complexity.

He is the proverbial Tower in a deck of tarot cards, a dynamic force which destroys that which no longer serves. We may attempt to cling to the vestiges of old situations and constructs lay festering, even to the detriment of our own health and sanity. Set, once we allow him into our lives, does not allow this to happen.

We are no longer afforded the luxury of laying in the dysfunctional comfort of our own demise. The dynamic force is set into motion, and our lives are never the same for it. Toxic relationships crumble to dust, houses of cards fall, and only through strength, awareness and surrender will we have an understanding of what is actually happening; the process of true liberation.

Through my connection with Set, I went through this alchemical process - through our meeting on the astral plane, I spontaneously took on the role of Osiris, and what followed was my harsh spiritual dismemberment and re-birth. I felt the dull pain within my etheric body as Set cut me to my core in swift, efficient slashes, with no trace of anger or malice.

After the ritual, my life started to change. I had always had an open and inquisitive mind in life, and had never simply inherited my views, beliefs and expectations from others.

Much has been revealed throughout my spiritual journey, but my ritual work with Set took these qualities to a whole new level. I began to question society further still, and my place within it. The illusory nature of our third dimensional world became ever clearer to me, and it soon dawned on me what I will and will not accept from the prescribed societal structures and herd mentality which surrounds us. My mental place and calibration within my nation, my race, my gender, all dissolved. It was an egoic transmutation.

I soon came to find that I needed space to integrate these new experiences, and so I re-arranged circumstances in my life to be able to gift myself that much-needed space and solitude.

I became more emotional, and also empathic to the energies and emotions of others. Sounds in the outside world also became too loud for me. I became sensitive to the energy leakage which occurs all around us on a daily basis. Silence is what I yearned for, and that is what I gave myself.

The shifts were not without pain, but as the dross of my life was systematically cut away.

What I was left with was a newfound strength, and a clearer understanding of myself and my true desires in life, regardless of the societal structure that I happen to exist within. A transmutation had occurred, and is indeed still occurring.

In my understanding of the ancient Egyptian myth, it is clear that Set was the dynamism and driving force that set the foundation for Osiris' rebirth and renewed glory and strength, through the ritual dismemberment and scattering of his body. Liberation through suffering and death. Like many such accounts of gods and deities from civilizations past, it is a true allegorical model of the power which lies in the balance and integration of polarities. A model of power which can be tapped into and experienced by the modern-day magician.

I feel that the antinomianism of his gnosis is a powerful key which unlocks the binds of our spirits and minds. It takes courage and fearlessness to see these changes through, and we may choose to invoke the qualities and strengths of the Lord of the Desert to stay within our power.

I feel that there are still many of the spiritually inclined who fear and shy away from these darker themes. It is a fear of the unknown, an old and decrepit programming which has outlived its use.

It is my understanding and experience that the shadow self must be acknowledged, accepted, and integrated if we are to truly grow in spirit and strength. To deny our very own shadow is to halt our healing.

Resistance and fear is what makes the journey painful. Surrender can be a great act of liberation. It is the difference between choosing to stand in the eye of the storm, or to choose to allow ourselves to get trapped and caught up in the chaotic debris of the external and illusory world.

There is a beauty and grace to The Fall, and this is a message which working with Set can reveal.

THE ROLE OF SET IN WESTERN OCCULTISM

Fra Diavolo

Introduction

In the eternal pantheon of the gods, the deity Set plays a special role. As generally known, or can be easily found through internet research, Set was originally an Egyptian desert god whose origin and appearance challenge us with some puzzles. The most common representation of Set is that with a human body and the head of a "canid," whereby to this day the experts do not agree on which animal head was actually represented. The assumptions range from a donkey over an aardvark to a giraffe or even an extinct animal today, which can therefore no longer be exactly identified.

Set and the Theory of the Elements

In Western Esoterism, a great significance is ascribed to the hermetic theory of the elements. In short, it describes the work of magic with correspondences to the four classical "basic elements" of Earth, Water, Air and Fire. Accordingly, the corresponding magical properties are analogous to the respective element and encompass all levels of being, from the material to various spiritual levels. For the element fire, for example, the corresponding qualities would be hot, bright, hot-blooded, irascible, chaotic, unstructured, strong-willed, and combative. A reference to the elemental theory of the Hebrew mythology is found in the holy name "Yahweh" YHWH, which is considered a mystical and magical Tetragrammaton, since Hebrew letters, beside the word meaning, are also assigned spiritual properties which refer to the name YHWH and its corresponding elements: Fire (Yod), Air (He), Water (Waw) and Earth (Heh). Set, because of the etymology of the name, is traditionally associated with the element of Fire and all its corresponding properties, with correspondences viewed differently throughout history, thus showing different aspects of Set. Positive fiery aspects that can typically be associated with Set are, for example, courage and fighting, Set as protector and warrior god. The Greek philosopher and writer Plutarch translated the name Set to "the overwhelming" or "the ruler." The negative properties of the Fire element were connected with his ability to create chaos and unrest. He was also said to rule over storms.

Set and the Kabbalah

The Kabbalah is a very important aspect of Western Esotericism because it is a kind of universal mystical and magical formula of manifestation. According to Jewish doctrine, the word of God is expressed with the help of the so-called Sephiroth, which represent various emanations of the divine creative power and are arranged on the Tree of Life according to a specific pattern. These Sephiroth are connected by 22 paths, which among other things represent the Hebrew alphabet.

The origin of the Kabbalah doctrine is the Sefer Yetzirah (Jetzira) of the Jewish mystery doctrine. At the beginning of the text the 10 Sephiroth appear alone and their meaning is explained without using the representation of the Tree of Life. This depiction probably originated in the Middle Ages in Europe and led to the image of the Tree of Life as we know it today. Through the system of the Golden Dawn, the Tree of Life became an integral part of the Western mystery doctrine, which resulted in various components being supplemented and extended by correspondences and equivalents of other systems. According to this system, the lower levels of the Tree of Life also represent the elemental levels, i.e. Malkuth = Earth, Yesod = Water, Hod = Air and Netzach = Fire. Thus, on a lower level, the element of Fire can be associated with the planet Venus as well as Netzach as a Kabbalistic equivalent on the Tree of Life. As already mentioned in the previous section, Set has a strong relation to the Fire Plane and is automatically assigned to the Netzach Sphere on the Tree of Life. According to the occult tradition, the Kabbalistic Tree of Life begins with Kether and the number 1 and ends with Malkuth and the number 10, with a crosswise descent to Malkuth, representing a flash. According to this numbering, the Netzach sphere has the number 7.

Following the Kabbalistic tradition of the Tree of Life, the opposing sphere is considered as an extension and completion of the corresponding level, which in the case of Netzach is level 5: Geburah, also corresponding to the planet Mars. Located diagonally opposite on the Kabbalistic Tree of Life, the sphere of Geburah expands the active and fiery aspects of the Netzach energies. If you add up the numbers, you get $7 + 5 = 12$ and the number $1 + 2 = 3$ as a cross sum.

The number 3 also brings the Binah sphere into play, which will be discussed later. But first, another important correspondence is to be investigated, namely the correspondence of Set to death.

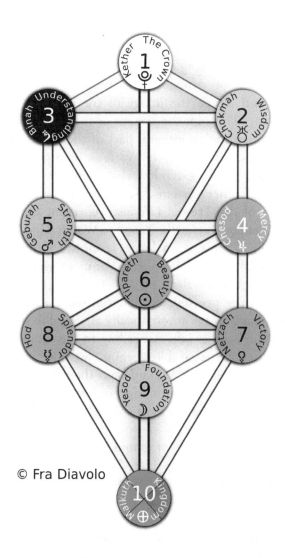

Tree of Life by Fra Diavolo

Set and Death

To find the connection between Set and death, there has to be taken a closer look at one of the innumerable myths about Set, especially the "Osiris myth." This story is about Osiris, the son of the god Geb and the goddess Nut, who symbolized heaven and earth in Egyptian mythology. These two deities had 4 children: Osiris, Isis, Set, and Nephthys. Osiris became the ruler of the rich and fertile Egyptian kingdom and married Isis. Set, in turn, gained control of the barren and hot desert of the South, which, of course, he did not like at all, so he tried to seize control of Egypt by murdering Osiris. Thus, in this myth, Set is associated with death by killing his brother Osiris to take his place, becoming the first god in Egyptian mythology to kill another god. In his essay: *Death, State, Cosmos: Dimensions of the Myth in Ancient Egypt,* the Egyptologist Jan Assmann takes it a step further by describing Set as the first one bringing death into the world and thus into the pantheon of the Egyptian gods. For him, this myth plays a fundamental role similar to the biblical fratricide of Cain to Abel. The role of the Death Deliverer is a turning point in the way Set is viewed, because with these remarks Assmann makes it clear that Set can be seen as more than "just" a rogue or adversary since he brings death into our lives. Of course, this is not necessarily physical death, but rather the death of stasis and solidification. The old is destroyed and gates are open for the new. Those who walk the way of Set, walk the way of renewal and development. In general, it can be said that on a transcendental level Set holds the function of the transformer by forcing changes to initiate a reorientation.

This feature, therefore, brings him inevitably in connection with the Saturn sphere, which in astrology and the Kabbalah has been considered to be the planet of fate since time immemorial. Interestingly enough, Saturn, like Set, has undergone a change in the course of his mythological history, since he was originally a god of agriculture in the Roman pantheon, but was soon equated with the Greek god Kronos. Kronos was the son of the divine couple Gaia and Uranos, who, like the parents of Set, symbolized heaven and earth.

Francisco Goya: Saturn Devouring His Son

According to the legend, Uranos threw all his children, called Titans, into Tartarus, the underworld of Greek mythology. From there, Kronos freed himself with the help of his mother Gaia and seized power and the throne by castrating his father Uranos with a sickle. The similarities to the myth of Set and

Osiris are evident in this legend, and Kronos (Set) takes on the role of the transformer and changer, too. If Saturn is related to the Hebrew Kabbalah, as shown earlier, then Saturn corresponds to the Binah sphere and therefore has the number 3. However, because Set should typically be located on the dark side of the tree due to his left-hand-path properties, the highest octave of his existence is the Qlipha Satariel, which is, so to speak, the dark side of the Binah sphere.

Set and the Qliphoth

There are many ways to look at the Tree of Death and the Qliphoth as the opposite side to the Sephiroth on the Tree of Life. At their core, these planes represent the dark and infernal primal forces, and the left-hand-path magician tries to use these forces on his path of magical development and accept and transcend them as part of his being to grow and reach a higher level of consciousness. Today, in our society, the dark side is considered as "evil" and needs to be eliminated. Due to the development of monotheistic religions over the millennia, one considers the unity with God as the only task and the right path of man. Because of this social pressure, however, a counter-movement of dissenters and individualists has formed in the course of time, which has reinterpreted the dark as something that symbolizes the personal and individual development of man and thus is considered as standing in opposition to society. Generally, the society represents a community which subordinates the well-being of the individual to the benefit of all. The symbol standing in opposition to this rule is the figure of Set as he typifies a counter-image in the pantheon of the gods and positions himself as an adversary to the socially recognized values. Symbolic of this is also the myth in which Set is not born like the other gods, but rips himself out of the mother's womb. Thus, Set has a clearly dark orientation and is associated with the Qliphoth as the Other Side (Sitra Ahra) of the Kabbalah. A possible connection between Set and the Qliphothic Tree of Death can be established by simply counting from the Malkuth sphere, which has the number 10 and corresponds to our material world, reaching the Tree of Death through 11 = Thaumiel, 12 = Ghagiel and 13 = Satariel - the Qliphothic equivalent of the Binah plane. The number 13 corresponds to the Crowley and Waite Tarot card "Death" and thus logically complements the above.

The Swedish occultist and author Thomas Karlsson writes in his book *Qabalah, Qliphoth and Goetic Magic* about the Satariel Sphere:

> "Satariel is the first Qlipha after the river of the Abyss. The adept enters into Satariel reborn and baptized in the black water of the Abyss. Satariel is the dark side of Binah, and these worlds are strongly related since Binah is already in itself a dark force that acts as a root of the left side on the Tree of Life. The difference is that Satariel is not part of the bright order of the Tree of Life, but part of the Sitra Ahra and the other side. Both Binah and Satariel correspond to the dark and mysteries. They represent the principles that carry all answers within but lie hidden in utter darkness. Satariel is the one who keeps secret and hides something. The darkness that is created in Binah acts as a negative form in which Creation receives its shape. Binah and Satariel represent time and destiny and are associated with goddesses of fate, like the Creek Moires and the Nordic Norns. The three Moires are Clotho, Lachesis and Atropos, and their task is to spin twine and cue the life thread of each and every man. Clotho holds the distaff and rules birth. Lachesis rules what takes place during life, and

Atropos, who wears a black veil, cuts the thread
that determines death."

In order to comprehend the deity Set in his totality and to
connect with him on a higher level, one has to embark on
the path of self-knowledge and self-transformation. This path
is a non-return path because it requires the adept to be
aware of all limitations and obstacles on one's way, to
transform and transcend them, and to recognize and accept
them as an expanding part of oneself to grow. Set asks us to
take over control and to ascend to the throne. This is not an
invitation to violence or hatred because it is about the "Self,"
Take control of your being and becoming, grow, be what you
want to be. Question the existing, start something new and
separate yourself from things that prevent you from growing,
this is the way of Set.

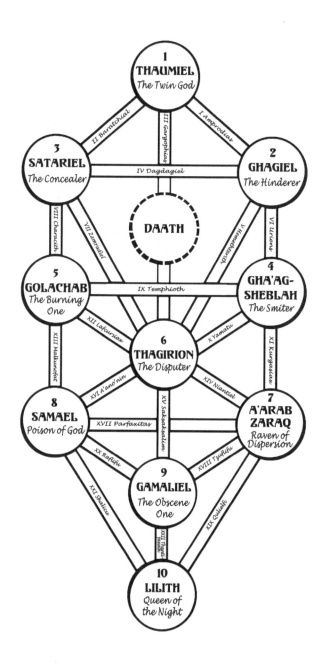

Tree of Qliphoth

THE RITUAL OF SET-TRANSFORMATION

Fra Diavolo

The aim of this ritual is to invoke Set in order to become aware of his strength and power and to use this power to transform the participant's being. The ritual is designed for 4 participants, with one participant invoking Set and the other participants supporting the invocant and experiencing the inner transformation through the invoked deity. The 4 as a number of participants symbolizes the 13 as a checksum of 1 + 3 = 4, as well as the number 4 as the number of manifestation of YHWH. Of course, the following ritual can be easily adapted to a different number of participants - for example, one person performing the role of several people. All people wear black robes, and, if possible, all participants have a dagger. Each person, standing at the triangle tip also holds a black candle (alternatively, the candle is positioned on a sufficiently high candlestick or simply on the ground).

Sacrament: A chalice of red wine or another red liquid, e.g. grape juice.
Incense: Kyphi, dragon's blood or frankincense.

A triangle is drawn on the floor (e.g. with chalk) or laid out (e.g. with fabric or tape) with the top facing South. The triangle should be large enough so that the participant invoking Set can comfortably sit in the middle of it. At each tip of the triangle stands one of the 4 participants (or more than 4 participants), holding a black candle. In the triangle you should also place the tools for the invocant: the mask of Set, in which at the height of the third eye on both sides (inside and outside) the seal of Set is drawn in red color (if no special seal of Set is used, a simple reversed pentacle will work as well), a dagger, a black candle and the chalice with the sacrament that the invocant has to charge while channeling the consciousness of Set, as well as the incense burner.

1. Opening

The room is darkened, but if necessary, a subtle backlight can be used. The invocant begins the ritual by entering the triangle, lighting the black candle in the triangle, burning the incense, raising the right hand with the dagger and pointing the index finger of the left hand to the ground. Then the invocant shouts:

In the name of the Great Dragon, we came here to call Set to this temple - Set! Look at us! Test our will!

Then the participants answer:

Set! Send us the mighty fire of the South to burn all enemies and strengthen our will.

The candle in the south is lit.

The invocant folds his arms over his chest forming the shape of a cross (pointing his right hand with the dagger upwards, left hand across) and shouts:

In the name of the Great Dragon, we came here to call Set to this temple - Set! Listen to us! Test our spirit!

The participants answer:

Set! Send us the storms of the East to blow away all the mental shackles in your raging waves and clarify our thoughts.

The candle in the East is lit.

The invocant lowers his arms and shouts:

In the name of the Great Dragon, we came here to call Set to this temple - Set! Connect with us! Test our power!

Then the participants answer:

Set! Send us the waters of the West to wipe away all resistance in your raging waves and to flood us with our inner strength.

In the West the last candle is lit.

2. Energy raising

The invocant sits on the chair or on the floor in his favorite asana. In front of him is the mask of Set on which the seal of Set is drawn. He activates the seal by gazing at it and starting a rhythmic breathing until the edges begin to blur and a slight trance occurs. At the same time, the other participants point their daggers or their hands in the direction of the triangle (without getting into the triangle), visualizing how a glowing dark red sphere of lava is forming around each tip of the triangle. They feel the heat and perceive the energy that radiates from the spheres.

The participants start chanting quietly the mantra "OMNIA INCIPIT - OMNIA TRANSIT (Latin: "everything starts - everything passes away") and direct the energy from the spheres (each participant concentrates on the triangle tip he is standing at) through their bodies and their hands toward the triangle, at the same time visualizing the triangle burning with fire. After a while, this fire becomes stronger and more intense until it becomes a wall of fire that blazes and radiates heat. Again, the participants focus on the energy that is being transmitted. It feels like an electric current that rushes through their bodies. When the invocant has activated the seal, he stands up, puts on the mask of Set and takes the chalice with the sacrament into his left hand and the dagger into his right hand.

3. Invocation of Set and Charging the Sacrament

The invocant is standing still, visualizing how Set manifests and connects with him through the activated seal on his forehead. At first, he becomes aware of the fiery-red eyes, then he perceives his hot breath surrounding him like fog. Finally, the dog-shaped head and the rest of the body forms, which then comes closer and finally merges with the invocant. Meanwhile, the other participants assume the posture of Set by placing their fingertips together with outstretched hands over the chest and spreading the arms at the angle of 45 degrees. At the same time, they visualize how Set manifests in front of the invocant. They focus all their attention on the image of Set, rejecting all other thoughts.

4. Transformation

When the invocation is complete, the invocant raises the arm with the dagger. This is the sign for all others to finish the visualization of Set. The invocant points the dagger to the chalice in his left hand and channels the energies of Set into the sacrament. Once the sacrament has been adequately charged, the invocant cuts open one side of the triangle with the dagger, breaking the triangle and vibrating: "I have brought myself to life - I have become the ruler of death and destiny." He lets every participant drink from the chalice and then takes a sip himself. Now all participants sit down in their favorite asana and the invocant goes back to the middle of the triangle and sits down as well. He now visualizes blood-red energy rays emerging from his body and connecting with each of the other participants through the solar plexus (Manipura Chakra). Meanwhile, the participants focus on their Manipura Chakra and the sacrament they have just drunk, visualizing how it begins to pulsate and gradually spreads throughout their bodies. After sufficient concentration, the participants connect with the energy of the sacrament and immerse themselves in the awareness that they are connected to the energy of Set. They watch all body reactions and mental visions that they feel or experience. The participants should become aware that they have absorbed the strength and will of Set, giving them the opportunity to redefine themselves, to start something new, to end the old, and to end the ritual as strengthened, strong-willed persons.

5. Dismissal of Set and End of the Ritual

As soon as the invocant senses that the energy of Set is beginning to fade, he ends his visualization and gets up. This is also the sign for the participants that they should return to their mundane consciousness and end their visualization as well. Finally, the invocant raises the dagger and shouts:

Let Set show us the path and our will shall be manifested!

The participants answer:

And so it is done.

BREAKING BOUNDARIES:
A SEXUAL ENCOUNTER WITH SET

Soror Sortela

Even within the Draconian Path, Set is not traditionally or symbolically associated with Sex and Sexuality. Usually, it is Lilith or Samael who are attributed with initiating the practitioner into the methods of sexual magick and revealing to them their deepest and darkest desires. However, Set represents Self-Becoming and overcoming any obstacles toward that goal, and the sexual encounter I am about to relate in this essay occurred within the context of overcoming the obstacle of Gender Identity and destroying the barrier between my male physical gender (which I came to no longer identify with) and the ever-so truthful realization that I in fact identified as a woman.

Obviously, such a tremendous and life-changing decision did not occur overnight during a single ritual, with a single deity, but was rather the culmination of various workings with different spiritual forces, the Qliphoth and Draconian Deities being only two examples. However, it was Set who sealed and concretized the entire process of realizing my Transgender Identity in a powerful and emotionally-charged initiatory experience, and thus I have chosen to focus on his role in my process of Self-Becoming.

Also, this did not occur during a single ritual, but culminated through an entire year's working with Set, where much gnosis of a mystical and practical nature was revealed, and so it is necessary to examine the most salient revelations during this one-year work with this adversarial deity.

A Name and a Book

My very first working with Set provided me with a secret name by which he may be effectively called forth, by chanting the name as a mantra. This may also be coupled with Kundalini raising techniques for maximum effectiveness.

The name itself is TANGAROS and the mantra is "Tangaros, Tangaros, Xeper Tangaros."

In all my personal workings with this Dark Deity I have employed this mantra with great success, and during one of our early communications he spoke to me through automatic writing this following "book" or "liber" that I now present here, not necessarily as a new gnosis or logos but rather to demonstrate the connection I was beginning to develop with Set and because it sheds light on his esoteric nature as destroyer of obstacles:

I break the tablets upon the crimson shore,
Alabaster and marble line the entrance to my temple.
I am the Terrible God of all-time, no time
to kill the Sun, he is already dead.

Aeons pass, I am the Silent One.
Spit upon the skulls of the dethroned.
Who cares for them? Not I.
You cannot break me, because I will break you first.
I speak to still, I still long to devour the world in Blood and
Fire and Deadly Venom.
Serpents serve me, so do the desert beetles, the foxes,
the crux of the Kingdom of Flesh.
Bear with me, come unto me not as a miserable sinner,
nor a servant, but a friend, an accomplice of Damnation.
Walk with me, beside not behind, in front is even better.
Apep smiles at my insolence, we are one, we are not
different.
Die in battle. Battle is the word of death. I give you no
other word, for Zain is upon us.
Break the flesh with swords. Steal the heart of love.
You will not readily understand, nor utter, yet I know you
will.
There is no hierarchy of Initiation. Will is All.
And yet there are fools who will treat this as sacred.
Fools! Nothing is sacred.
Only that which is done, that which will be.
I've underestimated you my scribe. I will elevate you
beyond the stooping pyramids.
Down, down into Tuat we go!
For therein lies the glittering pearl.
Are you afraid to die?
Don't be! What you will so shall you get. Mind shall perish.
Preserve the Body, and the Mind shall perish. Preserve the
Mind, then the Body perishes also.
Keep your will alive, constant, changeless,
and soon the Heavens shall be your domain.

The following invocation should be used in conjunction with
the mantra presented above, if one wishes to partake of their
own personal "dark" gnosis with the god of Self-Becoming:

O mighty Set,
Self-begotten, Eternal, Timeless!
I invoke Thee!
Tangaros, Tangaros, Xeper, Tangaros!
Burn away the illusions that imprison my soul,
obliterate the obstacles on my path of Ascent
with Fire and Force and Dark Desire,
Lead me to the Throne of the Silent God,
The Great Initiator of the Crimson Desert!
Be at my side, behind and before,
Bring sleeping wisdom to the fore,
O Set, thou Self-Created God,
Abide with me here and now!

The Philosophy of Self-Becoming

The following passage consists of a brief outline of the philosophy embodied by Set. A brief commentary follows.

0. Only vulgarity betrays the Way of Waste.
- So Behold! -
1. Philosophy precedes Magick.
2. All methods and practices must be justified by the Logico-Erotic Consciousness, by the Supreme Will - and not slavishly adopted like the scholars of outdated grimoires do.
3. Seek, Obtain, Destroy, Rebuild - and all systems spring from the Primal Gnosis of the Mother Dragon.
4. All-Knowledge exists at All-Times, and the Void-Way is forever achieved.
5. Even if "proven" wrong, deny! Only that which is Willfully-established is "valid". Thus, if there was a god and one were to meet him face-to-face, vehemently deny this Salvation, and be cast out to the Nightside where you will be welcomed openly as King and Conqueror.
6. This is the Way of Waste, the Ultimate Rebellion.
7. Seven Seals, broken, open to the Limitless Vault ETERNAL.

The Commentary

"Vulgarity" refers to non-academic and daily vernacular to express primal magickal axioms. Magick is certainly not limited to the ritual space, but rather permeates every instance of human life, and so even the most seemingly-mundane words, actions, and events betray deep magickal truths. The Draconian Magician seeks to imbue his or her entire existence with Magickal Sight, and to use his or her abilities to achieve their will within the world. It is for this reason that Philosophy, both magickal and academic, is an essential tool in the training of intellect and the refinement of one's perception of metaphysical truths - necessary prerequisites to the successful application of force, momentum, and craftiness to realize one's goals.

The second verse is a criticism against previous schools of the Right-Hand Path, who present the candidate with a series of pre-established religious dogma that must be adhered to regardless of otherwise demonstrable contradictions. On the Draconian Path, the Initiate must rely exclusively on their intuition and personal experience to draw their own conclusions regarding timeless metaphysical queries, rather than rely on some "holy scripture" to show them why and how magick ought to be employed.

This leads directly into the next verse, which provides its own self-explanatory comment upon the previous statement. The Draconian Magician must employ creativity and imagination in order to successfully craft rituals proper to channeling the deities of the Draconian Path and for the successful invocation or the Qliphothic Shells and Tunnels. The often-ridiculous instructions for crafting magickal implements and for conducting a "proper" evocation found in the Solomonic grimoires can easily be classed as outdated and metaphysically obsolete, since the Judeo-Christian tradition has lost much of its previous vitality and significance.

The essential keys to successful magick, as previously mentioned, are Creativity and Imagination (Desire should also be mentioned as a necessary motivation) for without these fueling the ritual work of the Magician the results will be haphazard at best, negligible at worst. Furthermore, in this age of rapid scientific advancement and increasing skepticism toward faith-based religions, it would be a complete mockery to one's Logic and Intellect to "believe" in any sort of Supreme Being that ought to be worshipped. In the Draconian Path, the Magician is his or her very own God/Goddess-in-the-making, and only reference to one's own undeniable intuition should provide the metaphysical map by which he or she classifies and organizes spiritual phenomena. The writings of the German philosopher Friedrich Nietzsche ought to be read in conjunction with these statements. Likewise, within the context of this essay, the reader would profit from a perusal of Albert Camus' voluminous treatise on rebellion: *The Rebel.*

Only by applying philosophical common-sense and refusing to follow blindly any religious dogma can the Magician rebuild his or her own magickal universe. Such is the essence of Verse 4.

Verse Five is the quintessential premise and "proper attitude" to be adopted by the practitioner of the Left-Hand Path. Even when proven "wrong", if one's previous views were sound and well-founded upon reason and logic, then one should by all means stick to them, and not falter or fold in the face of any "higher" man. This stubborn and staunch refusal to submit or bend to the will of another is a primary characteristic of the Draconian Adept.

At last, the final two verses poetically seal the previous affirmations and close the *Hymn to Rebellion.*

The Sexual Encounter Itself

Obviously, due to the very personal and intimate nature of this experience, I will be brief in regards to the details of what occurred during the ritual itself. Rather, I will explain how I benefited from engaging in astral sexual intercourse with Set.

Basically, Set taught me how to employ my body in a feminine manner, whether through aesthetic decorations such as makeup or through selection of clothing, to appear more womanly, and to entice and attract members of the male sex. He also taught me how to sway my hips to be able to walk in a more feminine manner. And finally, during the act of copulation itself, in which I transformed my astral body into that of a woman to allow Set the capability to penetrate me on the astral plane, I had the opportunity to experience female orgasm and sex from a woman's perspective.

To conclude, if it wasn't for that one night with Set I would not have been so resolute and convinced of my Transgender Identity and have the intellectual and practical tools whereby I can confirm and ground this Identity on the Physical Plane. For that, I am indebted to Set for destroying the boundaries of traditional gender roles and allowing me to explore my ever-so growing feminine side.

THE FLAMING STAR OF SET

Asenath Mason

The following set of workings was conducted as an open project by the Temple of Ascending Flame in October 2014. It is centered on Set, one of the primal Draconian gods, his fiery current powering up the path of flames, and his role in Luciferian magic as it is viewed in the philosophy and praxis within the temple.

The project contains 7 workings which have to be done on 7 days in a row, at any hour of the evening/night. They are designed to attune your consciousness to the current of the Dragon by assuming the god-form of Set - the powerful and self-created Lord of the Left Hand Path. The first working opens the gateways for the energies of Set to enter your consciousness, making further work with his current possible. The following five days are dedicated to exploration of the five psychic senses by assuming the Draconian form of Set. The last day's ritual combines the work of the whole week into a powerful invocation of the current of Set. The purpose of the project is to introduce the practitioner to the mysteries of Set as the Lord of the Inner Flame through the work of his Flaming Star representing the five "Dragon" powers that are awakened, activated and developed through the self-initiatory Draconian magic.

About Set

Set is an archetype of the Adversary, the God of Storm and Change, the principle of dynamic transformation. He is an ancient Egyptian deity, originally the god of the desert, the scorching rays of the sun and the patron of outlanders. The exact meaning of his name is unknown, but it is often translated as "one who dazzles," "pillar of stability" or "one who is below." As a god of the desert, Set was related to sand storms and deadly powers of the sun. Because of the extreme desert climate, he was considered a very powerful deity, one of the main gods in the entire pantheon, and he was also the patron deity of the Hyksos dynasty who worshipped him as the chief god. His other names were e.g. Setesh, Sutekh, Setekh, Seti, Suti, Set-Heh, and Smai. Because of the word "Tesherit," which in Egyptian means "desert" and is very close to the word "Tesher," meaning the red color, Set came to be associated with all that was red - red desert, red sun, red flames, and red hair with which he was often depicted in art. His most familiar depiction, however, is that of an unknown animal or Typhonic beast with a curved snout, square ears, forked tail, and canine body, which bears no resemblance to any known animal.

In Egyptian myths of the underworld Set was the defender of Ra during his journey through the realm of the dead, slaying the enemies of the Sun God every day while travelling with him in the Barque of Millions of Years. Apart from being a powerful and dangerous deity, Set was also a benevolent god, often associated with sexuality and virility. He was also a friend of the dead, the crowner of pharaohs and the patron god of soldiers and warriors. With the appearance of the well-known story of Osiris and Isis (he killed Osiris and dismembered him so that he could not be resurrected) Set came to be associated with violence and disorder and became the Adversary. The Greeks identified Set with Typhon, the primordial dragon-monster, and attributed to him such phenomena as eclipses, thunderstorms and earthquakes. In this sense, he embodied the forces of chaos as opposed to forces of natural order. For this reason he was also often identified with Apep (Apophis), another primordial serpent. In other myths, Set himself fights the serpent together with other gods who assist the Sun God in his journey to the underworld. As the opponent of Osiris, he is a symbol of strife and dynamism as opposed to comfort and stagnation. As the one who defeats Apep, he is the emblem of triumph over blind chaos. One of his names is Set-Heh, meaning "Eternal Set." This represents his function as the Initiator of the Path to Infinity, the one who awakens the Dragon force within and lifts it to the stars so that man may become one's own creator. Therefore, he is one of the most powerful archetypes of the Lords of the Left Hand Path. He is not born in a natural way but he rips himself violently out of his mother's womb - tearing out his way to manifestation as a self-created being. He slays Osiris, which is symbolic of the defeat of stasis and shattering of old thought patterns, the triumph over death itself. His fiery nature represents lust, fury and passion - the force of desire which is the driving force on the path. Finally, his Flame is the Divine Fire, the inner spark of Godhood that through the work of the Left Hand Path becomes the fiery pillar of ascent.

Set is usually depicted as a man wearing a red mantle with an arrow-tail and the head of his zoomorphic beast, but in ancient depictions he was also shown as a crocodile, donkey, snake, jackal, hippopotamus, scorpion, pig, and several other animals associated with his mythology. These many forms reflect his primordial nature, as it was thought that he was born without a definite shape. Amorphous beasts, shapeshifters, and beings of multiple forms are usually associated with the Void as they reflect the chaos and mutability of the primordial substance that gave birth to all creation - the Womb of the Dragon. The zoomorphic shape that will be explored within this project is the serpent. Snakes in ancient Egyptian myths usually represented a form of chaos - either creative, like Kematef, or destructive, like Apep, and had both protective and deadly powers. They protected the deceased who traveled through the underworld and guarded the gates to each division of Amenti. Chthonic animals were mysterious and sacred to the ancient Egyptians as they were believed to come into existence without a creator. They were thought to be self-created. Serpents had a special position as they also shed their skin, thus being regarded as symbols of rejuvenation, rebirth and resurrection. In Egyptian iconography we often find depictions of the God-Creator in the form of the Great Serpent, sometimes with wings, legs and a human head. This serpent represents the eternal principles of death and birth, creation and destruction. He is eternal and infinite as he existed before all creation and will remain after all creation is destroyed. The serpent is the beginning and the end of time. In an esoteric sense, it is Kundalini, the evolutionary force that is the foundation of all life and the source of immortality. Here we will invoke the serpent SATA in his creative and annihilating aspect, reflecting the polarity of life and death within the Serpent Force/Kundalini as it is manifest within the current of Set. SATA is a serpent dwelling in the underworld, known for his regenerative and protective powers, a symbol of new life and resurrection. In the *Papyrus of Ani*, he speaks "I am the dweller in the uttermost parts of the earth. I lie down in death. I am born, I become new, I renew my youth every day." His Qliphothic counterpart is the negative, or shadow side of this Ophidian/Draconian force. They both constitute the Eye of Set that is the focal point of the whole project.

The Flaming Star of Set is a form of the Pentagram of Set. The pentagram itself has a wide symbolism and many associations within various cultures, magical traditions and ritual systems. While the upright symbol traditionally represents the triumph of spirit over matter, the inverted star is associated with "evil," the Left Hand Path, dark and sinister magic, and the reversal of "the proper order of things." It is a symbol of Baphomet, the goat of black magic, whose horns are represented by the two upper points of the pentagram, the ears by those on the right and left, and the beard by the lowest point at the bottom. It is the symbol of the Devil, the Adversary and the antinomian path "against the natural order." Also, its five points have been attributed to many different concepts corresponding to the number five and its symbolism. In our work, the five points of the pentagram represent the five psychic senses in the "Dragon body" of the practitioner, corresponding to the five senses in the physical body. These five "Dragon senses" are accessed through five flames that burn at the particular points of the pentagram. Awakened and activated, they form the sixth flame, which is the Inner Flame that within the Setian tradition is known as the Black Flame, the symbol of isolated consciousness on the path of self-deification. The pentagram is also a symbol of the soul entering the underworld, or in a metaphorical sense, descent into the subconscious, the very core of the Self, where the Inner Flame is ignited in the self-initiatory process on the Path of the Dragon. One of the magical symbols of Set is the letter *Sh* or *Shin*, which is the letter of fire, the spirit and the Fire Snake Kundalini that stands for the driving force behind all evolution. This is the primal force of the Dragon that powers up the ascent of the Initiate. Combined with *Teth* (snake), the letter *Shin* forms ShT, the name of Set, who presides over this process in the Draconian Tradition. "Set" or "Sut" also means "black," and his color in rites of magic is either red, symbolic of his ancient mysteries, or black, representing the underworld.

The sigil used in the project represents the Eye of Set, which is a manifestation of the Eye of the Dragon, the symbol of awakened consciousness. The Eye is formed by SATA, the serpent of the underworld, in his double aspect, representing the cycle of death and birth in rites of passage that are part of the initiatory process. The inverted star is not constrained by any boundaries as it stands for isolated consciousness. It points down, showing that the focus of the initiatory formula is toward the within - descent into the personal underworld of the Initiate. The core of the pentagram should be red, representing the red setting sun and the direction of west which is the gate to the Current of Set.

Before the Rituals

Prepare your ritual space in the way you feel is suitable for this work. On your altar you may put statues, images or other sigils that represent Set - these can be ancient depictions, modern images, or simply your personal seals or drawings. You may also choose to focus on the sigil alone, without any other decorations - this choice is entirely up to you. The sigil is provided further in this text - you can print or draw it yourself and it has to be big enough to gaze into comfortably. If you wish to paint it, you can use colors associated with Set and his Draconian Current: red and black - this can be a red seal on a black background or black sigil on red - but the central part of the sigil, which should be red, has to stand out of the picture. Apart from the sigil, you must have a large pentagram on the altar - this can be a drawing, a piece of cloth with a pentagram on it, or you can make a pentagram e.g. of wood. It has to be in the central point of the altar, big enough to place five candles at its points and one candle in the center. You will also need five red candles - these have to be placed at the points of the pentagram, and one black candle, representing the Flame of Set, to be placed in the center. The black candle will be burning all the time, the red ones will be lit separately, each in a different working. Therefore, it is recommended to use candles of two different sizes, e.g. a large black candle and five small red ones - so you may comfortably focus on one at a time without being distracted by the flame of another.

DAY 1

Opening the Gates to the Draconian Current of Set

The Eye of Set

Put the sigil of the Eye of Set in front of you and sit in a comfortable position. Light the black candle that represents the Flame of Set and burn some incense. If you need more light in the room, feel free to have more candles, but do not use the five pentagram candles yet. For the workings of this project you can use Dragon's Blood incense or the Nile Temple. If you use music for meditation, the recommended choice is Emme Ya *Hau-Hra - Hymns ov Adoration to Seth-Apep.* Anoint the sigil with a few drops of your blood and focus all your attention on it. You can also anoint your forehead on the Third Eye. See how the lines of the sigil become charged and activated with your life substance. Visualize it glowing and flashing with the fiery energies of

Set, with the core of the sigil turning red, coming alive, burning and swirling like a vortex.

At the same time, speak the words:

In the name of the Dragon,
Primal Source of All Creation,
I open the gates to the Current of Set,
Here in this temple and within the depths of my soul,
And I invoke the Lord of the Inner Flame,
The Red One,
The Furious One,
To enter my being and become as one with me,
As I become as one with him.
Shta-t shep ari khet.

Then focus on the sigil again and chant the following serpent names as a mantra:

SA-TA AT-NE-SA

This has to be chanted slowly, in a low whispering voice - like the hissing of a snake. Keep gazing at the sigil until you can easily memorize and visualize its shape. Then close your eyes and recall the image in your inner mind. Focus your inner sight on the shape of the sigil, see it forming in front of you, in the black space, burning with fierce red flames. At this point you can keep chanting the mantra or continue the practice in silence. Continue to see the sigil forming in front of you, burning and flashing. The serpents that form the Eye become alive and move, hissing the same names you have been chanting. Envision the sigil changing, shifting into other shapes, unlocking the gateways of your mind, opening the doors to the Nightside, and showing you objects, entities, landscapes, and scenes. Let the visions flow freely and open yourself to the experience. Send the message through the sigil and ask Set for his presence and guidance on the path of flames, invite him to your ritual space and the temple of flesh. Feel his fiery breath flowing through the sigil that is now a living gateway to his current. And finally, envision yourself in the center of the burning pentagram - the Flaming Star of Set that is now around you, and you are the central point of it. When you feel it is time to end the meditation, return to your mundane consciousness, blow out the black candle and finish the working.

This working may bring visions of the desert, ancient temples, pentagrams morphing into other shapes, and Draconian beasts - snakes, dragons, lizards, or reptilian creatures composed of many different animal parts. Flames are all around and you may feel both as being surrounded by fire and experience the fiery heat arising from within. This is accompanied by physical and tangible phenomena - candle flames flickering, growing and moving with a mystical wind, temperature rising in the room and the sound of hissing coming from all around. The vision of the desert is a recurring motif here as well. It is dark and bright, black and red, hot and cold, empty and full of spirits and animals. You may see it as a gloomy and haunted place - with skeletons, skulls and rotting corpses. It is also full of sounds and noises - the hissing of snakes and the howling of desert beasts. It can be devoid of any life, or you may see temples and places of worship, corridors of burning pillars with black snakes coiling around each pillar spitting venom to feed the flames, pyramid temples standing at the edge of the abyss, steps and tunnels leading up and down, pyramids with the Eye of Set in between and on the top, tombs with pillars among the desert sands, black-golden buildings with the Pentagram of Set on the floor, and constructions with the statues of the god. You may experience sensations connected with the extreme climate of the desert: the chill of the night and the infernal heat of the day. You may also see the whole realm in blood-red colors: the red sand, the crimson sun rising in the west and setting in the east, red bones of primordial giants lying scattered among the sands, etc.

The serpent SATA manifests here alone or with other serpents. Sometimes the other snakes are parts of his body and his emanations. You may have visions of being surrounded by snakes, some of them coiling around you, others writhing on the ground, and you can feel transformed into a serpent yourself - moving and hissing like a snake, swaying and dancing to the hypnotic music of the desert. Other visions characteristic of this work are those of a huge mass of snakes or tentacles. They may manifest in front of you and pull you inside or enter your body and devour you from the inside. Visions of reptilian snake or dragon eyes are common in this part of the ritual as well - they appear above, instead of the sun in the sky, or below, generating a vortex of energy that merges with the practitioner.

Set is usually seen in this working in his ancient Egyptian depiction with the Set-animal head. He also often appears as a temple statue - with red glowing eyes and snakes coiling around him. His energy flows through the statue, or the statue eventually becomes alive and transforms into another form of manifestation. Sometimes he is seen sitting on a throne, his face like in ancient Egyptian depictions. Other times he has a human face and flaming red hair. There are also visions in which his face is only hidden behind the animal mask, while his body is that of a tall and muscular man. The face behind the mask may not be seen, though, as it is shifting and morphing, never staying long in one form - reflecting his primordial origin and essence - bestial and human, alien and familiar, monstrous and beautiful. Sometimes he has a scepter in one hand and ankh in the other, and other times he is holding flames or fiery serpents. Communion with his energies is accompanied by visions of sitting on his throne and thus acquiring his powers, receiving his scepter and ankh, being touched on the Third Eye or all chakras to awaken the flow of energy, or being given his mask to put on the face - thus receiving access to his senses. Sometimes he is also seen with the burning pentagram around him or above his head. Finally, he can be seen simply as a part of the whole scenery in which he manifests - primordial darkness, pure and without form.

DAY 2

Invocation of the First Flame

The purpose of this ritual is to invoke the Draconian Current of Set to awaken and activate the first psychic sense: Clairvoyance. It is represented by the first flame of the pentagram that is ignited in this working through the meditation of the first candle.

Psychic senses are the equivalents of the five physical senses. They are called "Clair Senses," the name being derived from the French word *clair* meaning "clear." This corresponds to the Draconian principle of "clear seeing" and the etymology of the word "dragon" (in Greek *drakon* means "to see clearly"). Awakened and activated by the Serpent/Dragon Force (Kundalini), these psychic senses replace the physical, thus developing and empowering the subtle body of the Draconian Initiate. Clairvoyance is the psychic equivalent of sight or vision. It attunes the "inner sight" to extrasensory vibrations of energy, making it possible to "see" without the aid of the physical eyes. This ability is experienced through impressions beyond the limitations of mundane perception, remote seeing, visions of the past, present and future, and interactions with beings that exist on other planes and in different dimensions.

Begin this working in the same way as the day before: prepare the temple, light the black candle and burn incense.

This time, however, light the first candle - at the left upper point of the pentagram (the order in which the candles should be lit is marked in the image below).

When this is done, envision yourself in the center of the Flaming Star of Set again. The fire is all around you and you are the central point of the pentagram and the whole ritual. Breathe deeply and slowly. Feel how the flames move and grow with your breath. At the same time, feel the fire rising within - from the soles of your feet, through the spine, up to the top of your head. Take as much time as you need to build this image in your mind. When you are ready to continue, speak the words of invocation:

Lord of Flames,
Mighty Sutuach,
Let me pierce the veil of the night with your sharp sight!
Show me what I need to see,
And reveal to me the wisdom of the Other Side!
My eyes are open and I receive what you choose to show
me!

Then sit in a comfortable position and focus all your attention on the flame of the candle. Again, chant the mantra of calling: *SA-TA AT-NE-SA*

At the same time, visualize the sigil forming in the flame and growing bigger and bigger until it becomes a large gate in front of you. It is fiery and you can feel the hot breath of Set flowing through it. You can also hear the hissing of snakes, and shortly after, two fiery snakes emerge out of the red core of the sigil and enter your body through the eyes. If until this point you meditated with your eyes opened, close them now. Stop chanting. For a moment you can feel them burning and then your physical sight is shut off and your attention moves to the inner sight. Your inner eyes open and you can see the world with the Dragon sight. If you wish, you can use a physical aid here, e.g. a blindfold. Your eyes are now the Dragon's Eyes. With your piercing gaze you can see through barriers and illusions of the world. Look around, explore this feeling and observe the differences in your perception of the surrounding room and its objects. See them glowing with their own light, vibrating with energy. See the energies of the Draconian Current of Set pouring into the room through gateways that are now shattered by your flaming gaze. When you feel it is time to end the meditation, close the working and return to your normal consciousness.

This working is simple but powerful and even if you have never worked with such practices before, you should still experience a significant enhancement of the sense of sight and be able to perceive astral energies, shapes and colors in a natural way. You may have visions of the Desert of Set in this working as well, but the main focus here is transformation into the Draconian form of the god, thus acquiring his senses and merging your consciousness with his. This can be experienced in several ways. You may see yourself as the god himself - with his attributes, ancient Egyptian clothing and ornaments, or with his animal mask. You may also experience transformation into one of his Draconian beasts - serpent or dragon. This is accompanied by acquiring the primal reptilian consciousness - the sharp sight that can pierce the substance of reality, see through it and gaze in all directions, with no limitations of the body. For some practitioners this transformation is very realistic and tangible and they see themselves moving in their snake form in a serpentine way, in a hypnotic dance, or gliding through dimensions. Others fly through the space in the form of a dragon or winged serpent. Those who experience a glimpse of Set's divine consciousness describe it as a feeling of being in the center of the universe, observing all places and all events at the same time. It is also not uncommon to simply focus on the inner sight and see the surrounding room and objects as glowing and vibrating with their energy, fire burning on the floor, eyes observing them through the flames, and the fiery energy taking shapes of pentagrams, stars, inverted triangles, hourglasses, blades, etc. Finally, you can visualize the whole sigil being projected on your forehead, thus awakening the Third Eye and the sense of the inner sight. The whole experience may also include burning sensations and the increase of temperature in the ritual space.

DAY 3

Invocation of the Second Flame

The power of the second flame is Clairaudience. It corresponds to the physical sense of hearing and is based on the perception of sound. In the Dragon body this refers to perceiving sounds and extrasensory vibrations with the "inner ears." This psychic sense is closely connected with Clairvoyance and usually they both are developed at the same time.

Like the day before, start the meditation with preparing the temple, lighting the black candle and burning some incense. Do not use music for the meditation - it might be too distracting to perform this practice properly. This time light the second red candle - at the lowest point of the pentagram.

Again, envision yourself in the center of the Flaming Star of Set, following the same visual meditation. Take as much time as you need to build this image in your mind. When you are ready to continue, speak the words of invocation:

I call he who speaks with a million of voices!
Mighty Sutuach,
Voice of the Storm!
Come to me with lightning and thunder,
And whisper to me the wisdom of the night!
My ears are ready to receive your message!

Then sit in a comfortable position and focus all your attention on the flame of the candle. Again, chant the mantra of calling: *SA-TA AT-NE-SA*

Visualize the sigil forming in the flame and growing bigger and bigger until it becomes a large gate in front of you. See the flames that form the gate and feel the hot breath of Set flowing through it. Like in the previous meditation, you can now hear the hissing of snakes, and shortly after, another two fiery snakes emerge out of the red core of the sigil, this time entering your body through the ears. At this point stop chanting. Close your eyes and focus all your attention on the sense of hearing. For a moment you can feel your ears burning and bursting with a cacophony of sound, then your physical sense of hearing is shut off and you can hear the sounds around you with your inner ears. If you wish, you can also use a physical aid here, e.g. ear-plugs. You ears are now the Dragon's Ears. With your sharpened sense of hearing you can receive auditory sensations that are normally not available in the mundane condition. You can hear voices of gods and spirits that answer your call through the planes. You can explore the art of remote hearing and try to attune to other people or places. You can interact with beings that exist in other dimensions. Their language may be translated by your consciousness as sounds, noises or visual sensations - such as glyphs or symbols. Let it happen. Explore your new power and enjoy the experience. When you feel it is time to end the meditation, close the working and return to your normal consciousness.

This working is usually described as more difficult than the practice of Clairvoyance, but even with little experience you should still be able to perform it successfully. For many practitioners this is an exercise to control their internal dialogue, opening themselves to sounds and clairaudient sensations of the astral plane. Also, many people experience physical sensations during this work, such as burning or itching of the ears, and sometimes even pain when the fiery snakes merge with their consciousness. At first, you can also have various clairaudient sensations - muffled sounds, noises, singing, chattering from the other planes, whispers, hissing, etc. - rather than actual words or messages that can be distinguished and understood. As your mind gets attuned to these noises, opening up to the experience, you will be able to hear sharp and clear sounds from all around - voices and sounds from the neighborhood, at first random, like conversations popping out of nowhere, but then it will be possible to choose what to focus on. This is sometimes so clear that some practitioners can even hear the heartbeat of people in the nearby surroundings. If you are really successful in this practice, you will manage to attune your "inner ears" to the sounds of the Desert of Set and the voices of other planes and dimensions. These sounds include ringing, whispering, singing, strange music, wailing and screaming, buzzing, howling, hissing, wind blowing and whispering messages, etc. You can also hear the voice of Set talking to you. What is interesting to note, is that the sounds and noises of the other planes are often translated by the mind of the practitioner into the most familiar means of communication, such as visual sensations. In this case, the sounds may be perceived as forms, shapes, glyphs, and sigils - whispers and voices crystalized into images - and in this part of the project it is very likely to receive sigils and other messages in a graphic form, especially if you are a visual rather than auditory person.

DAY 4

Invocation of the Third Flame

The power of the third flame is Clairscent. It is the psychic equivalent of the physical sense of smell. In the Dragon body this is the power of perceiving odors or fragrances that are either not in the practitioner's surroundings or transmitted through other planes and dimensions. Each entity or a place/realm manifests not only with visual imagery or sounds but also often with a characteristic smell. These smells are usually beyond the borders of normal perception and only a small portion of them is received through the physical nose. Psychic perception is not limited to physical organs, therefore the scope of senses used in a magical experience is taken beyond all these limitations.

Like the day before, start the meditation with preparing the temple. Light the black candle, but this time do not burn incense - you need to focus on the psychic sense of smell, therefore try to eliminate physical smells from your surroundings. Light the third red candle - at the right upper point of the pentagram. Then envision yourself in the center of the Flaming Star of Set, and when you are ready to continue, speak the words of invocation:

Mighty Sutuach,
He who sits enthroned in the temple of darkness,
Grant me your sharp senses and make them strong!

*Let me smell the fragrance of the sweet incense burned in
your temple,
And lead me through the desert with the hounds of the
night!*

Again, sit in a comfortable position and focus all your
attention on the flame of the candle while chanting the
mantra of calling: *SA-TA AT-NE-SA*

Visualize the sigil forming in the flame and growing bigger
and bigger until it becomes a large gate in front of you. See
the flames that form the gate and feel the hot breath of Set
flowing through it. Again, this is all accompanied by the
sound of hissing, and shortly after, two small fiery snakes
emerge out of the red core of the sigil and enter your body
through the nose. At this moment you may feel that you
cannot breathe, gasping desperately to catch a breath. Let it
happen and do not panic. Stop chanting. Close your eyes and
focus all your attention on the sense of smell. After a while
you will feel that your physical sense is shut off and the whole
realm of extrasensory fragrances is now open for you to
explore. Do not focus on your physical nose. Instead, try to
attune your inner sense of smell to the energies around you.
Also here you can use a physical aid - something that will
block the nose while trying to breathe through the mouth -
but this is quite unnatural and you may find it too
distracting. It is rather recommended to focus on receiving
the olfactory perceptions through the mind, without paying
attention to any physical organs. Focus on the flame and let
it be your channel to the wonders of the Nightside - feel its
distinctive smell and envision that it carries also something
else - the odors and fragrances of other realms and their
denizens. Explore the power of the Dragon smell which is
sharp and sensitive, like the senses of beasts that can smell
their prey for miles, but yours is even stronger - you can
smell everything in the entire universe. Places, other beings,
things from beyond the barrier of time and space - all these

visions are now enriched by a multitude of smells. Enjoy the experience and when you feel it is time to end the meditation, close the working and return to your normal consciousness.

Like in the case of the previous workings, you may experience physical sensations when the fiery snakes enter your body and merge with your consciousness. These are usually difficulties with breathing, after which the inner sense of smell becomes attuned to odors and fragrances of the astral plane, either rapidly or in a slow entrancing way. Many practitioners experience the smells being translated by their minds into images, like auditory sensations. These smells are mundane and familiar, including e.g. herbs, flowers, forests, the ocean, the smells of the neighborhood, etc. Other smells seem to come from other planes and materialize through the inner senses of the practitioner. These are the smells of the desert - sand, hot air, temple incense, etc., as well as smells such as sulfur, burning fire, sexual fluids, and blood. The smell of blood is a recurring motif in this working as well. Some practitioners describe it as thick and metallic, sweet and fresh, sometimes mixed with sexual fluids, other times carrying the stench of decay and putrefaction. Others experience the smell of blood with visual sensations, such as sitting in a pool of fresh hot blood, its smell mixed with aromatic incense and ancient Egyptian visual symbolism. If you are successful in this practice, you may experience the multitude of smells in the whole universe, discovering that everything has a smell, odd and different than experienced with the physical sense, sharp and clear in many unusual ways. You may also experience transformation of the human sense of smell into a strong, atavistic, bestial consciousness, and before diving into the world of odors and fragrances, you may see yourself being transformed into an animal - werewolf, snake, dragon, or another Draconian beast. In this case, the perception of smells is mixed with the sharpened senses of the animal consciousness.

DAY 5

Invocation of the Fourth Flame

The power of the fourth flame is Clairgustance, which corresponds to the physical sense of taste, or gustation. It is the ability to perceive the essence of spiritual and ethereal substances through "taste." This psychic ability is not given as much attention as the others, but if properly developed, it opens the practitioner's mind to a wonderful synaesthesia of senses in which the visual and auditory perception is combined with a wide range of tastes and flavors.

Again, start the meditation with preparing the temple, light the black candle and burn incense. However, you may also choose to work without incense in this ritual, as taste and smell are closely related and they are often experienced as one. Light the fourth red candle - at the left lower point of the pentagram. Then envision yourself in the center of the Flaming Star of Set, and when you are ready to continue, speak the words of invocation:

> *Greatest of the Gods,*
> *Mighty Sutuach,*
> *Taste my blood as I taste yours through this sacred communion,*
> *Transform my senses into those of a beast of prey!*
> *Let me hunt with you under the cloak of the night,*
> *And fill me with your essence as we become one!*

Follow the same pattern of work - sit in a comfortable position and focus all your attention on the flame of the candle while chanting the mantra of calling: *SA-TA AT-NE-SA*

Visualize the sigil forming in the flame and growing bigger and bigger until it becomes a large gate in front of you. See the flames that form the gate and feel the hot breath of Set flowing through it. Like in the previous meditations, this is all accompanied by the sound of hissing, and shortly after, two fiery snakes emerge out of the red core of the sigil, merge into one and enter your body through the mouth. Open your mouth to let it happen. Stop chanting. Close your eyes and focus all your attention on the sense of taste. Do not shut off the other psychic abilities that have already been activated: sight, hearing and smell. Instead, try to combine them all by adding the sense of taste. Your mouth has become the Dragon's jaws and you experience the world around with the sharp senses of Set. This is deeper and more profound, opening you to tastes and flavors you have never experienced before. You can now drink the essence of the moon and the sun, taste the sweet and bitter substance of the currents that flow through the gates of the Nightside, and interact with the dwellers of other realms and dimensions through a communion of senses. Even tastes that you already know seem different, experienced on a completely different level. Explore this power and enjoy the experience. When you feel it is time to end the meditation, close the working and return to your normal consciousness.

This working is usually described as the most difficult of all as the sense of taste is rarely explored through ritual practice and many practitioners do not pay attention to this psychic ability. However, if you manage to succeed in this practice, you will experience the "taste" of substances and energies of other people and objects on a completely different level than in the mundane consciousness. Again, this is at first accompanied by physical sensations and many practitioners report difficulties with breathing, choking and even an urge to vomit while the fiery energy enters their bodies through the mouth. Sensations experienced in this work include such tastes as bitter, sweet, sour, metallic, etc. - rich and thick in texture. The taste of blood is a common motif as well, and it affects the mind of the practitioner in a very intense way, releasing animal instincts and awakening bestial consciousness. Sometimes this feeling is accompanied by the vision of transforming into a beast - this time the snake-form is the most common - and you may even see yourself with a forked tongue of a snake. Those who manage to awaken the sense of taste and fully enjoy the experience, usually describe it as tasting all things in the universe - air, wind, various objects, and living beings. This tasting of energies of other people is sometimes described as a very intense and unusual experience, and it opens access to a lot of things, not only the energy but also what the person sees, feels and thinks in a particular moment - thus "tasting" the whole essence of a living being on a completely different level than what it usually means in the mundane sense.

DAY 6

Invocation of the Fifth Flame

The power of the fifth flame is Clairtangency, known also as "clear touching" or psychometry. This form of extrasensory perception corresponds to the physical sense of touch. In magical work this ability makes the visual experience tangible, as subtle impulses and vibrations of energy are "translated" through the sense of "touch" into physical impressions, which creates a bridge between a psychic manifestation and a physical experience. This ability is also used to obtain information about objects or their owners by touching them, which is also known as object reading. The sense of touch is usually associated with the palms of the hands, but it is actually experienced through the whole skin, thus affecting the entire body. In rites of magic this ability especially becomes useful if we summon the energies from other realms and dimensions to manifest on the physical plane.

Follow the same pattern of work - prepare the temple, light the black candle and burn incense. Light the last red candle, at the right lower point of the pentagram - it represents the fifth flame that is explored and merged with the other Dragon senses in this meditation. Again, envision yourself in the center of the Flaming Star of Set, and when you are ready to continue, speak the words of invocation:

Lord of the Black Flame,
Mighty Sutuach,
Make my body strong and my will invincible,
Grant me the power to reach to the stars,
And touch me with your tongues of fire!
Sutuach, I stand before you ready to receive your power!

Like in the previous meditations, sit in a comfortable position and focus all your attention on the flame of the candle while chanting the mantra of calling: *SA-TA AT-NE-SA*

Visualize the sigil forming in the flame and growing bigger and bigger until it becomes a large gate in front of you. See the flames that form the gate and feel the hot breath of Set flowing through it. Again, this is all accompanied by the sound of hissing, and shortly after, two fiery snakes emerge out of the red core of the sigil and enter your body through the palms of your hands. Stretch out your hands with palms upwards and let it happen. Stop chanting. Feel the fiery Draconian Current of Set spreading from your hands over the whole body, setting it on fire which burns inside and fills your aura with the flaming essence. Combine this feeling with the other senses awakened and activated through the workings of the previous days. They are now the Dragon's senses, a manifestation of the primal Draconian force of the Void. Become as one with these senses and explore how it feels to be a living manifestation of this primal current. Let Set, the Lord of the Flame, guide you through this meditation. See the universe with the eyes of Set and experience the world with his sharp senses that are not limited by any physical constraints. Explore these powers and enjoy the experience. Open yourself for whatever it may bring. When you feel it is time to end the meditation, close the working and return to your normal consciousness.

This experience is usually described as intense and producing strong physical sensations. These sensations include heat, electric vibrations and tangible manifestation of energies. Sometimes they are so strong they are almost painful, accompanied by visions of being bitten by snakes, pierced by sharp blades, or transformed into another shape - more suitable to channel and process the flow of this flaming current. Other times they are pleasant and entrancing, sensual and intoxicating, awakening every inch of the body. During this working it is also common to experience either the ecstatic feelings of power or disappointment with the limitations of the physical body which is not adjusted to feel the totality of the invoked force. The fiery serpents entering the body through the palms of the hands are experienced as streams of flaming energy that merge and flow through the spine, producing visions of transformation and shape-shifting. Again, the snake-form is the most common, as well as the winged dragon-form. The flow of energy is also felt as a hot desert wind and waves of heat burning the body from the inside. You may also see your arms and hands transforming into snakes - and while you can extend your hands to touch anyone, e.g. use your normal hands for reading someone, the snake-hands can be used for attacking a target, thus revealing new aspects of this interesting and powerful skill.

DAY 7

Ritual of the Flaming Star

This ritual combines the workings of the previous days with the invocation of Set that unites the Dragon powers awakened and activated through the meditations of the five flames into Set-consciousness, the living manifestation of the Draconian Current. The ritual framework is here similar to the previous workings, but this time all five Dragon senses are invoked and combined with what is usually known as the "sixth sense," which is "feeling" within the whole body, or in other words - the full experience of Set-consciousness.

Prepare your temple like on the previous days - light the black candle and burn incense. This time light all five red candles marking the five points of the pentagram. Focus all your attention on the sigil and at the same time chant the mantra of calling: *SA-TA AT-NE-SA.* Again, envision the sigil glowing and flashing with the fiery energies of Set, the red core of the sigil coming alive, burning and swirling like a vortex. See the other participants around. Feel the fiery breath of Set flowing through the sigil, his presence behind the gates of the Nightside, awaiting invitation to enter your consciousness. Feel your body being charged with this fiery energy, vibrating and filling you with the Draconian essence. And finally, envision yourself inside the burning pentagram - the Flaming Star of Set that is now around you. You are the central point of it and the whole ritual.

When you are ready to continue, speak the words of invocation:

Xeper-i-Set! Nuk neter, nuk Set, ur!
Pert em kerh, Sutuach!

I invoke you, Mighty Set!
Lord of the Red Desert!
He Before Whom the Sky Shakes!
Voice of Thunder!
Strongest of the Gods!
The Furious One!
Come forth from the Void, from the Lair of the Dragon,
and ignite your flame in my soul!
Lord of the night, whose breath is the scorching heat and
the penetrating cold of the desert,
Arise with storms and tornadoes and fill me with your
fearsome power,
Show me how to burn my weaknesses and destroy all
obstacles that stand in my way!
Give my eyes clear vision,
Give my voice the power of thunder,
Give my arms your strength,
Fill my heart with courage and my thoughts with clarity,
Awaken my senses,
And lead me on the path of self-creation!

I invoke you, Sutuach!
Xeper-i-Set!
I become as one with you and you become as one with me!
Your senses are mine, and I am your memory.
Grant me your feelings for this rite!
Guide me as I walk the path of the scorching desert heat!
Xeper-i-Set! Nuk neter, nuk Set, ur!
I am the lord of storms and the bringer of fire,
I spread my Dragon wings and I emerge from the Womb of
Darkness,
Forming myself by my will alone!
I am the blade that cuts through the stifling web of
stagnation and inertia,
I am the lust and fury that shall not be constrained,
I am the untamed force that shakes foundations of the
universe,

And I am the flame that turns man into god!
I am Set!
I am the Self-Created God!
Ho Ophis Ho Archaios!
Ho Drakon Ho Megas!

When you finish the words of invocation, focus again on the burning pentagram around you. At first, follow the same procedure - breathe deeply and slowly and feel how the flames move and grow with your breath. This time, however, take a step further - visualize that the fire of the pentagram moves toward you from all around, enveloping you in the flaming essence, entering your body through the skin and all your senses - you can see, hear, smell, taste and touch it - it is alive and moving. At the same time, feel the fire rising within - from the soles of your feet, through the spine, up to the top of your head. And finally, envision that you *become* the Flaming Star yourself. There is no other fire - you are the only flame - alone, powerful and unique. This is Set-consciousness. Explore how it feels to be Set - see with his eyes and open yourself for anything that may happen. Let the experience flow freely and spontaneously. Observe the temple and sense phenomena which manifest in the ritual space when Set comes through the gates of the Nightside, or close your eyes and let him manifest and speak to you through your inner mind. If you do not experience any tangible manifestation or concrete visions, it is still recommended to write down all thoughts that you may have after the working and meditate on them. Take a look at your visions and experiences from the whole project and meditate on your previous and future steps on the path. Let this final day be the time of reflections and perhaps new inspirations on the Path of the Dragon. Finish the working with the traditional closing:

And so it is done!

The last day should bring reflections on all five senses, combining them into one experience. This working is usually described as powerful and vivid, expanding consciousness and making the senses sharp and awakened. Visions are here similar to those in the previous workings - Set and manifestations of his Draconian current in the form of fire, snakes, stars, and pentagrams, images of the desert and ancient Egyptian temples, and sensation of being transformed into a living vessel for the Draconian current - assuming the god-form of Set, transforming into a winged dragon or fiery snake, or simply becoming one with this primal Draconian consciousness. This merging of consciousness with the current of Set is also felt as fiery snakes rushing through the body, being consumed by flames or huge flaming serpents, projecting consciousness into the Eye of the Dragon in the center of the Void, and many other intense chakra and Kundalini sensations, in which either the sigil of the Eye is projected on the practitioner's forehead or the Third Eye is seen as the center of the Flaming Star. There are also visions of putting on Set's mask and thus acquiring his consciousness. This consciousness is experienced as a feeling of being in the center of worlds and dimensions from which it is possible to see any place or person in the universe. These images are brought forth before the practitioner, while the god-like consciousness itself remains in the center of all. If you are successful in this work, you may also experience the true meaning of "Dragon Seeing," which is not about being able to travel or gaze into an already manifest reality but bringing it forth into manifestation right before the eyes of the practitioner.

This working also comes with many personal insights inspired by the whole project and reflections on the practitioner's individual progress. During and after the project you may observe the increase of energy in your day-to-day life, new inspirations in your personal work and enhancement of your magical skills. This energy is active and dynamic, bringing changes and insights, opening ways and removing barriers and obstacles, revealing new priorities and possibilities. It will affect your psychic senses and inspire you to work harder on transgressing your personal barriers and limitations. The whole ritual also brings powerful manifestations of fire and flames as well as sensations of heat - both the physical heat in the temple and the fire burning within, flowing through the body and enflaming consciousness. You may have a feeling of being liberated from the bonds of the flesh, ascending to the stars, flying above the body, or becoming the center of the space between worlds and dimensions. Finally, the Flame of Set will manifest as a force burning to ashes all that stands in the way of your spiritual progress, strengthening your will and determination and awakening new desires and aspirations on the path.

THE MANY FACES OF SET

Asenath Mason

This set of workings is a continuation of *The Flaming Star of Set* and includes the concept of the pentagram as the central focus of the whole work as well. It was conducted as an open project for the temple in May 2018. The workings are dedicated to Set, the self-created Lord of the Left Hand Path, and his many masks and faces that are assumed by the Initiate on the Draconian Path in the process of self-deification. Here we will explore five of them, but there are many more which you will encounter, or perhaps have already encountered, through your personal work with this ancient and multifaceted god-form.

The project contains 6 workings which have to be done on 6 days in a row, at any hour of the evening/night. As Set is the Prince of Darkness and his energies are naturally accessed at nighttime, it is not recommended to do the workings during the day. The purpose of the project is to awaken the consciousness of Set, the powerful archetype of self-deification, by assuming his chosen masks and exploring the role he performs for the Initiate on the Path of the Dragon. This is a self-initiatory work of inner transformation and self-empowerment. The first working will open the gate to the current of Set, attuning your consciousness to his energies. The following five workings will invoke the consciousness of the god in his chosen forms and aspects, i.e. the Isolator, Lord of the Desert, Initiator of the Inner Flame, God of Storms, and the Watcher, allowing the practitioner to experience and absorb his powers and qualities in the process of self-deification.

The Pentagram of Set

The pentagram of Set (see page 70) is the primary symbol of the Lord of Darkness. In *The Flaming Star of Set* we explored the five points of the pentagram as representing the five psychic senses in the "Dragon" body of the practitioner, corresponding to the five senses in the physical body. Awakened and activated, they formed the sixth flame, which is the Inner Flame that within the Setian tradition is known as the Black Flame, the symbol of isolated consciousness on the path of self-deification. The pentagram itself is also a symbol of the soul entering the underworld, or in a metaphorical sense, the descent into the subconscious, the very core of the Self, where the Inner Flame is ignited in the self-initiatory process on the Path of the Dragon. In this project, we will use the pentagram as a focal point of the rituals as well, this time placing the chosen masks of Set in its five points and the practitioner in the center. This will set up the ritual space and provide a sort of a magic circle for the communion of energies, establishing the magician as the central point of the whole operation.

The Sigil of Set

The sigil used in this project refers to Set as the Adversary, the God of Storm and Change, the principle of dynamic transformation, and one of the most powerful archetypes of the Lords of the Left Hand Path. It shows him rising in flames from an inverted pentagram, which refers to the Initiate on the path of fire using the Serpent Force as a vehicle of ascent. The eye in the center of the sigil represents the Eye of the Dragon, the center of awakened and self-deified consciousness.

Items needed for the project

- **The sigil of Set** (It should be printed or drawn on paper or another material of your choice, preferably in black color on a red background or in red on black. Make it big enough to gaze into comfortably, without straining your eyes.)

- **The pentagram** (You need to perform the workings within the pentagram, therefore you can either draw it on the ground or on a piece of cloth or another material that you can put on the floor and sit comfortably within. If you have experience with astral magic, you can simply create the pentagram around you on the astral plane.)

- **Five black candles** (Each one represents a different mask/face of Set. Light only one in each ritual, except for the first working, when you will need all five. Place them around you in five points of the pentagram.)

- **Strong, aromatic incense** (Dragon's Blood, the Nile Temple, frankincense, myrrh, or another fragrance of your choice.)

- **A tool to draw blood** (This can be a dagger, knife, razor, lancet, etc., and it is enough to draw a few drops only, no larger amounts are needed. The blood of the practitioner is a vital component of this work as it opens inner gateways within your consciousness and serves as a symbolic act of self-sacrifice, leaving place for initiation and transformation.)

Feel free to prepare the ritual space in the way you feel is suitable for this work. On your altar you can place statues or images representing Set - these can be ancient depictions, modern images, or simply your personal seals or drawings. You may also choose to focus on the sigil alone, without any other decorations - this choice is entirely up to you.

Other tools that you use in your daily work or in your personal work with Set can be included as well.

DAY 1

Opening Gates to the Current of Set

Light all five candles and stand or sit in the center of the pentagram. Put the sigil of Set in front of you and gaze at it for a while. Anoint it with a few drops of your blood and focus all your attention on the image. See how the lines of the sigil become charged and activated with your life substance. Visualize it glowing and flashing with the fiery energies of Set, morphing into a gate for the current of Set to enter your temple. At the same time, chant the word: *"Setnakt"* (Set is mighty) as a mantra, silently or aloud.

Keep gazing at the sigil until you can easily memorize and visualize its shape. At the same time, visualize that the pentagram around you burns with fire, protecting you from all that does not belong in the ritual space and making the mundane world fade and drift away. When you feel that the atmosphere in your ritual space has changed and is charged with the energies of Set's fiery current, speak the following invocation:

In the name of the Dragon,
Primal Source of All Creation,
And by blood and fire,
I open the gates to the Current of Set,
And I invoke the great Sut-Hek,
The Red One,
The Furious One,
Lord of Storm and Change,
The Isolator and the Watcher,
Lord of the Desert,

And Initiator of the Inner Flame.
Answer my calling and enter my being!
Guide me on the path of isolation and power!
And dwell here in this place that is the temple of my mind!
For I am your son/daughter.
I have wandered through the night to find you in the depths.
I am Erbeth and I walk the path of earthquakes and thunder,
I am Bolchoseth and I dwell within the Seven Stars,
I am Pakerbeth and I order my own Becoming,
And I am Set-Heh - eternal, isolated and mighty in magic!
Set dwells in my heart,
And I am Set.
XEPER-I-SET!
In Nomine Draconis,
Ho Drakon Ho Megas!

Then, close your eyes and focus on your inner sight. Breathe deeply and visualize that the pentagram burning around you moves and morphs as you breathe - the flames move toward you as you inhale and move away when you exhale, each time becoming higher and brighter. And finally, you are surrounded by a fiery wall that moves and breathes with you. Envision that from this fire emerges Set, the self-created god. He is black and dressed in gold garments, with the bestial mask covering his true face. In his hand he is holding the Was scepter, the symbol of power and dominion, and he hands it to you, inviting you to embrace his power. Ask him to guide you on the path of self-initiation and open yourself to whatever he may show or tell you. When you feel it is time to end the meditation, return to your mundane consciousness, extinguish the candles and finish the working for the day.

DAY 2

The Isolator

The purpose of this working is to experience the consciousness of Set as the Isolator - the primary initiator on the Left Hand Path, the path of self-creation. This mask of Set refers to the myth in which Set does not wait to be born in a natural way, but tears himself violently out of his mother's womb. In this tale, Set is the third of the four (or five) children of Nut, the goddess of the sky and the mother of the gods. Instead of being born in the normal manner, as his siblings were born, he rips his mother's womb and emerges to the world as a self-created being. From the LHP perspective, this provides a powerful model of self-initiation. This mask is represented by the first flame of the pentagram, and symbolically, by the black candle at the first point (see the image of the pentagram).

Begin this working in a similar way as the day before: prepare the temple and light the candle - this time only one - at the left upper point of the pentagram. Keep the sigil of Set close as well, and if you wish, anoint it with your blood to strengthen the connection. This is not necessary, though, because the sigil is already active, but you may do so if you choose. Again, envision yourself in the center of the burning pentagram. Breathe deeply and slowly. For a while focus on how the flames move and grow with your breath and feel the fire rising inside you - from the soles of your feet, through the spine, up to the top of your head.

When you are ready to continue, speak the following invocation:

Mighty Sut-Hek,
First among the gods,

Isolator and Initiator,
Enter my being and become one with me,
For I seek to become one with you.
Guide me on the path of self-creation,
And teach me the mysteries of Becoming!
Make my Will strong and fill my heart with Desire!
Setnakt!
Set is Mighty!

Then sit in a comfortable position and focus all your attention on the flame of the candle. Envision that it grows and morphs, eventually forming into the shape of Set himself. He steps forward and hands you a knife, Pesh-Khent, which is one of his symbols. The Pesh-Khent knife in ancient Egypt was used to cut the umbilical cord and to open the mouth during the Opening of the Mouth Ceremony. Therefore, it is connected with mysteries of both birth and death, which are a part of the initiatory process on the Left Hand Path. It is a symbol of birth and rebirth, destiny and isolation. Use it to cut the ties to all that binds you to the mundane world so that you can enter the Night of Set pure and liberated from what confines you in your life. Take as much time as you need for this meditation. At the same time, envision yourself as Set - let his energy become your energy, his senses become your senses, and his power become your power. Feel this force flowing through your veins and his thoughts filling your mind until you feel that you are one with him. At this point let the vision flow freely and open yourself to whatever may come. When you feel it is time to end the meditation, take a few deep breaths, extinguish the candle, and finish the working for the day.

Observe how this consciousness may affect you after the ritual as well - your thoughts, emotions, the way you see the world around you, and so on. The very purpose of this work is to initiate a change in your consciousness, so keep an open mind and let the consciousness of the Isolator transform you as you should be transformed.

In this working, Set usually manifests in his fiery form, with the Set-animal mask covering his face and in an ancient Egyptian outfit. He is black, but his eyes are fiery and shining. His knife is used to cut away all that binds you and keeps you stuck in your life or on your magical path. These can be people, things, or situations, but also emotions, such as fears, needs, desires, and expectations. This is accompanied by observations on how freeing yourself from your own perception of things changes the way they affect you. For most practitioners this is not about cutting the links to things existing externally, but cutting away their own emotional attachments. This is often a feeling of being in the center of the universe - in the Void or in a spider web - and seeing all that ties you to the external world, thus being able to cut what needs to be cut and leave what empowers your path, feeling pure and liberated from the confines of your own perception. These links may grow back, though, and it is often the beginning of a process that may take a longer time.

DAY 3

Lord of the Desert

In this working you will invoke the Lord of the Desert. The word "desert" in the mysteries of Set has many meanings and can be interpreted in a number of ways. In ancient myths, Set is the lord of all that is alien, hostile and threatening. The desert in this sense is seen as a place of the scorching sun and sandstorms that bring death to humans and animals as opposed to the fertile soil and waters of the Nile represented by such deities as e.g. Osiris. In the Qabalah, "the Desert of Set" is a term associated with the Abyss, and in this interpretation it is a place of desolation and emptiness - the Void. It is also connected with absence of all that is considered as safe and familiar, which puts the Initiate through harsh tests of will, integrity and persistence. All this and much more can manifest while working with Set as the Lord of the Desert.

Again, begin this working by preparing your ritual space, and light the second black candle - at the lowest point of the pentagram. Focus for a while on the sigil of Set, connecting with his current, and visualize yourself in the center of the burning pentagram. See how it moves and grows with each breath you take, and feel the heat rising within you as well. When you are ready to continue, speak the following invocation:

Great Sutuach,
Lord of the scorching sun and the red desert sands,
God of outlanders and all that lies beyond the world as we
know it,
Powerful and isolated,
Enter my being and become one with me,
For I seek to become one with you.
Guide me through the desert into the core of your inner
sanctum,
Overcome my weakness with your strength!
Fill my heart with courage and my mind with persistence!
And let me find my true self as I come into being!
Setnakt!
Set is Mighty!

When you finish the invocation, sit in a comfortable position and focus all your attention on the flame of the candle. Again, envision it growing and morphing, eventually forming into the shape of Set - the red Lord of the Desert. He steps forward, opens his mouth and devours everything around you - the temple, the surroundings, and finally the whole universe. You are now alone in a dark and empty space, where nothing exists and all comes into being. This is the Desert of Set, the Void, the Womb of the Dragon. Think of all that stands in your way to achieving what you want on your magical path. Let it form into shapes in front of you and then dissipate in the blackness that surrounds you. Think of all that you want to achieve and give it form, manifesting it in front of you on the black canvas of the Void and embracing as part of your newly created world.

Take as much time as you need for this meditation. At the same time, envision yourself as Set and feel this force flowing through your veins and his thoughts filling your mind until you feel that you are one with him. Open yourself to whatever he may show you and go wherever the vision takes you.

When you feel it is time to end the meditation, take a few deep breaths, extinguish the candle, and finish the working for the day. Again, pay attention to any manifestations of this consciousness in your day-to-day life following the ritual.

In this manifestation, Set usually appears as a giant being - sometimes he is a serpent, and other times a dragon. Visions of his ancient Egyptian appearance are common as well, but they seem less "human" and more primal and atavistic. He comes to the temple devouring everything around the practitioner, and finally devouring the magician as well.

This working also triggers thoughts of personal taboos and limitations, doubts and fears, and individual inhibitions. It brings forth visions of things to achieve and personal goals, and the practitioner is shown how to change and shape the surrounding reality.

DAY 4

Initiator of the Inner Flame

This working is focused on Set as the Initiator of the Inner Flame. This is a modern interpretation of his role in the initiatory process on the Left Hand Path. The Inner Flame, or the Black Flame, is the center of consciousness within the Initiate, and it is also the source of power and god-like potential within each human being. This corresponds to the Dragon's Fire or the Serpent Force in the Draconian Tradition and Kundalini in Tantra. In this mask, Set is viewed as he who ignites the spark of self-awareness and awakened consciousness, successively testing the Initiate to develop it into the flame of self-deification. As the Serpent Force awakens and becomes active, the Inner Flame becomes the source of illumination and liberation from illusions of the material world, and it eventually transforms the Initiate into a god-like being.

Like on the previous days, begin this working by preparing your ritual space. Then light the third black candle - at the right upper point of the pentagram. Again, proceed as before: focus on the sigil of Set and connect with his current, and visualize the burning pentagram around you. When you are ready to continue, speak the following invocation:

Invincible Set-Heh,
Great-In-Magic,
Eternal Set,
He who ignites the flame of godhood in the heart of man,
Enter my being and become one with me,
For I seek to become one with you.
Guide me through the darkness of ignorance to the light of wisdom,
Illuminate my way with your everlasting blaze,

Destroy my weakness with your strength,
And fill my entire being with your living fire!
Setnakt!
Set is Mighty!

When this is done, sit in a comfortable position and focus all your attention on the flame representing the third mask of Set - Initiator of the Inner Flame. See how it grows and morphs, eventually forming in front of you into the shape of Set. He steps forward, opens his mouth and breathes out a fiery snake, and you open your mouth as well and receive it. Envision the snake coiling around your spine, generating heat that rises in waves, successively spreading over your whole body and transforming it - burning all that is weak in you and forging what remains into a powerful structure. Focus on the center of this fire - perhaps it is the heart, the head, or another part of the body - or maybe the center is somewhere else. When you find it, focus all your attention on it. Meditate on the power radiating from your inner center and feel how it makes you strong, invincible on your path, persistent and determined in your actions, and successful in your projects. Envision yourself as Set and feel how his consciousness empowers the inner flame even more. Embrace all that may come to you with this experience and take as much time as you need for this meditation. When you feel ready to end the working, take a few deep breaths, extinguish the candle, and close it. Like with the other masks, pay attention to how this consciousness manifests in your day-to-day life following the ritual.

The energy in this working is violent and fiery. You may experience it as sexual and accompanied by many explicit visions, or it can just be a very intense Kundalini raising, with the fire moving up through the chakras and empowering them in its ascent. Many practitioners describe a concentration of this energy within the solar plexus, but it can also be focused in the heart area, radiating fire that surrounds the whole body with a protective sphere. This fire is a shield sheltering the practitioner from any harm on the path as well as a tool to burn all personal weaknesses. Most practitioners describe this working as a strong centering practice, leaving no place for external influences and making them strong in their core.

DAY 5

God of Storms

In ancient Egypt, Set was thought to be the god who created strange, unexplained and terrifying phenomena of nature, such as earthquakes, eclipses, and heavy thunderstorms. His hieroglyph was used in such words as "confusion," "turmoil" or "rage." In later times he was identified with the Greek dragon/serpent Typhon and in many spells included in the Greek Magical Papyri he appears as Set-Typhon. In modern interpretation, his ability to send storms and create earthquakes can be used by the Initiate to create a change in one's environment. In this sense, Set is the enemy of stagnation - he who sets things in motion. This is also connected with the myth of Set slaying Osiris, which in Setian mysteries is interpreted as a destruction of stasis for the sake of progress and change. In this working, you will invoke the God of Storms for the same purpose: to shake the world around you and create a change for something new to manifest.

Again, start by preparing your ritual space. This time light the fourth black candle - at the left lower point of the pentagram. Then proceed as before: focus on the sigil of Set, connect with his current, and visualize the burning pentagram around you. When you are ready to continue, speak the following invocation:

Mighty Set-Typhon,
Sender of storms,
Bringer of thunder,
Boiler of the waters,
He who stirs the depths to motion,
Enter my being and become one with me,
For I seek to become one with you.
Shake my world and set it on fire so I can burn what no
longer serves me!
Show me how to create and destroy!
Give me the victory over my enemies!
And teach me how to devour both men and gods!
Setnakt!
Set is Mighty!

Then sit in a comfortable position and focus all your attention on the flame representing the fourth mask of Set - God of Storm and Change. Envision it growing and morphing, eventually forming into the shape of Set. He emerges from the flames with the Was scepter and hits the ground beneath your feet, making it tremble. At this moment the fire around you ceases and the whole world shakes and starts falling apart. Nothing can withstand this force and only those things that truly empower your path remain. Think of what it means to you and take as much time as you need for this meditation. Envision yourself as Set and feel the power to create and destroy anything you want, change your life and shape it as you wish. When you feel ready to end the working, take a few deep breaths, extinguish the candle, and close the ritual. Again, pay attention to how this consciousness manifests in your day-to-day life following the ritual. The current of the God of Storms is violent and dynamic and it can manifest as such in your life - be prepared for it and willing to embrace what it may bring. Write down all that is relevant to this work and keep it in your records.

In this working Set appears with snakes or cobras. Sometimes he is surrounded by them, other times he holds them in his hands. Some practitioners see him throw the serpents on the ground and change them to lightning bolts that rip the earth beneath their feet. He is furious and fearsome in this manifestation, and the same feelings he inspires in the practitioner. This manifestation is so strong that you can actually feel the earth shake when his energy arises in the temple. He comes as a force of a tornado, destroying everything around you and leaving you in a dark place where you have to fight your "enemies" - disease, pain, depression, and other things that hold you back in your life. You may also have thoughts of sacrificing things on the path and moving forward.

DAY 6

The Watcher

This mask of Set is connected with the myth in which he appears as the watcher and defender of the barque in which the Sun God Ra travels through the underworld each night from sunset to sunrise. On its passage through the realms of darkness the barque is stopped and threatened by the serpent Apep who tries to swallow it. Among all companions of Ra, Set is the only deity powerful enough to kill the serpent and ensure the safe passage of the barque. In the same role he appears to the Initiate on the Left Hand Path - he is the remover of obstacles and protector of those who travel through the night. The slaying of Apep is also symbolic of the destruction of blind ignorance, delusional thinking and overcoming inner chaos for the sake of clarity and understanding.

Begin this working by following the same pattern - prepare the temple, light the black candle (at the right lower point of the pentagram) and focus on the sigil of Set. Gaze at it for a while to connect with his current and visualize the burning pentagram around you. When you are ready to continue, speak the following invocation:

Fearsome Set,
Protector of the Barque of Millions of Years,
Slayer of Apep,
Enemy of blindness and delusion
Strongest among the gods,
Enter my being and become one with me,
For I seek to become one with you.
Take me to your sanctuary of confusion and let me find clarity,
Bestow on me your sight so I may gaze through the night,
Open my eyes to truth and annihilate that which is not real,
And guide me on the way through the underworld of my soul!
Setnakt!
Set is Mighty!

Again, sit in a comfortable position and focus all your attention on the flame of the candle. This one represents the fifth mask of Set - the Watcher. Envision it growing and morphing, eventually forming into the shape of Set. He stands in front of you with his forked knife in his hand, surrounded by flames. Think of any issues you might have right now in your life and ask him to assist you in the process of resolving them. Visualize yourself as Set and let his consciousness guide you through this meditation. When you feel ready to end the working, take a few deep breaths, extinguish the candle, and close the ritual. Take a while to look back at your visions and experiences from the previous days and meditate on what they mean to you, how they affect your life, and how they empower your magical path.

This is usually a quiet working. You can use his knife to cut everything around you - all attachments and obstacles, and his scepter to set up goals for the future. This experience comes together with observations about obstacles on the path, seeing them as they arise and being prepared for dealing with them when they manifest. Once they appear in the working, Set devours them, making way for the practitioner to move forward on the path. This can be one particular "obstacle," visualized in this working and then removed or transformed with the energy of Set's current, or there are more things manifesting, drawing the practitioner's attention to where the effort should go at the moment. Many practitioners describe a feeling of being in complete control after this working, standing in their personal power and strengthened for whatever the future may bring. They also feel more distanced to daily issues and struggles, as well as more prepared to deal with them in a calm and balanced way. This is also what you can expect from this project. Your connection with Set will be strengthened and you may receive personal insights into further guidance on the path. The Set-consciousness will make you realize how to let go of things that hold you back, leaving time and energy for things that empower both your day-to-day life and your magical path.

SET:
AN ASTROLOGICAL
PORTRAIT

Bill Duvendack

For over a century, Set has been looked at extensively through an astrological lens, and 1 would like to take this opportunity to recap for those of you that may not be familiar with this material. As much as 1 cover here, more can be found in the writings of Aleister Crowley, Dr Carl Jung, and throughout many astrology books, specifically those that look at astrology from a more humanistic approach, encompassing universal archetypes and applying astrology to psychology, a modern trend in astrology. The myths of astrology are also useful to know.

Aleister Crowley first brought this into mass consciousness with many of his writings, in which he corresponded Set to Satan to the devil to the planet Saturn. In this article we will discuss these correspondences and explain how and why they are accurate and how they can be used for further magical success. Crowley writing about this didn't happen in a vacuum, though, and it could be argued that he was not the first to make this connection, either. However, his writings reached a mass consciousness level that others had not accomplished until that time. Let's start by discussing Saturn to see how these correspondences fit together.

Saturn

In astrology, Saturn has gotten a bad reputation over the centuries because it represents so many things that have to do with responsibility, maturity, lessons, and time. A brief list of correspondences include: responsibility, maturity and the maturation process, lessons, teaching, time, karma, foundation, stability, death, long-term growth, old age, and things that hold us back. To the ancients, Saturn was the last visible planet to the naked eye. It takes Saturn approximately twenty-eight and a half to twenty-nine years to go back to where it was at any given time. While usually this is put into context of a natal birth chart, you can also use this information without a birth chart. For example, if you have been at a job for twenty-eight years, then there will be a Saturn return having to do with said job. This can be a time of stabilization, grounding, lessons coming back around, and, if you have had success with that job, potential advancement.

Every person goes through a Saturn return at about that age in life. Every twenty-eight to twenty-nine years when Saturn comes back around, it brings with it lessons and epiphanies, yet sacrifices and opportunities, too. If you are over thirty, you know the profound impact that it will have. If you are younger than thirty, you are getting a glimpse into what to expect during that time of your life. However, this also means that Saturn comes back around at approximately age fifty-six or so, too. Let's face facts, though, we aren't the same people at that age than we were the first time it came back around the first time. The general rule of thumb is that when you're younger, Saturn takes away, but when you're older, Saturn gives back.

During my astrological career I have dealt with this for many friends and clients, and there are a few takeaways I would like to share that illustrate the profound nature of that time period. I know people that have lost their dream job around that time because they took it for granted. I also know people that have come into their dream job, too. I know people that have had their first child during that time as well. I know people that have gotten married around then, but also conversely, gotten divorced. I know people that have bought their first house then, as well as those that have lost their first house because they didn't honor their responsibilities. The basic premise is that there is the realization that it is time to mentally shift into a new, more mature, more serious approach to life. This is not an extensive list of what can happen during that time, but it does give you ideas to consider as far as knowing what to expect then.

However, at the second Saturn return, things are very different. The lessons of the second Saturn return have to do with wrapping up any loose ends in life because it is time to live the next part of life for you. Your obligations to society and family are done, and therefore you are freer to explore your own interests. In older astrology books, it was written that was the time to prepare your will and your estate because death was imminent. However, due to the fact that we live longer on average now, that idea no longer applies, even though it is something to consider doing anyway.

What about all of the years in between, though? Yes, Saturn is still active then, too, but in a different way. This does require some clarification of astrology, though. When a planet comes back to where it was it is called a return, and it is seen as conjunct or blended with its natal placement. The conjunct is also known as a conjunction, and is one of five major aspects in astrology. Aspects are based on angles and geometry, and they tell us how the energy is being exchanged between the bodies involved. The other four aspects are the trine, the sextile, the opposition, and the square. A trine is when a planet is one hundred twenty degrees from another, and is said to be a supportive but dormant aspect. If developed, long standing stability and positive success can be achieved. A sextile is present when planets are sixty degrees away from each other. This is known as a gently flowing relationship between the bodies involved, and usually manifests as a talent one has. An opposition is, you guessed it, when the planets are opposite each other, meaning they are one hundred eighty degrees away from each other. This aspect represents where tension is present. Finally, we have the square. A square is when planets are ninety degrees apart, and is a challenging yet opportunistic aspect.

While it takes twenty-eight and a half years to come back to its original point, Saturn makes all of these aspects at some point during one's life. During such times we can know what to expect, and can be proactive when it comes to our personal magical work and development through life in general. Let's break this down by using an example of your spiritual path. Whenever you made the decision to be more proactive with your spiritual growth, we could say that is the zero point or beginning point for our purposes. Here is the way to look at how the aspects come into play. At seven years into this cycle, you have a Saturn-in-the-sky-forming-a-square-to-the-natal-placement of Saturn. This is known as "transiting Saturn squaring natal Saturn," to use the proper astrological language. You already know what this means, you just don't realize it yet. If you know the phrase "seven year itch," then you have insight into what occurred during this time from a Saturn perspective. A seven year itch is a phrase to mean that every seven years you may get a desire or impulse for something new and/or different. This is caused by Saturn, and what is occurring is that Saturn is calling you to action and spurning you to adapt based on what your experiences have taught you. Then, the next aspect is at fourteen years, and this is an opposition between transiting Saturn and natal Saturn. This would have manifested as tensions on the path, or your dedication to the path causing friction in your daily life. However it manifested, it was a time of stress that produced growth. The next aspect would be seven years after that, when there is another seven year itch square to the natal placement. So, you could expect similar experiences and lessons to come up at this time that were at the first seven year itch. However, if you have learned what you needed to learn, the lessons that are brought to you are of a higher vibration than they were the first time around. But, if you didn't learn your lessons, then they will be just as brutal if not more so than the previous lessons. Finally, the next cycle is the full Saturn return, when it returns and comes full circle, conjunct to its natal placement where you find what we discussed above comes to pass. After the period of the return, which has its height of intensity for the first two years, you repeat the same seven year cycle application discussed earlier, and the lessons are repeated. If you got them right, they are more refined lessons on the same themes as before, but if you failed the earlier Saturn lessons, they will come back just as visceral as the first time, if not more so. After all, you're older, so you should be wiser, right?

You can see why Saturn gets the bad reputation it had for many centuries. Very few people are comfortable discussing themes of aging, death, and related concepts. I seem to remember that point in my life when I was internally, immaturely, rebelling against getting older, so I can relate to why people are uncomfortable, and Saturn is the planet that makes them uncomfortable, yet it represents the principle factor of life, which is that everything dies.

If you'll notice, in the above example I don't list the aspects of sextiles and trines between transiting Saturn and natal Saturn, so let's take a few minutes to do that here. You have a transiting Saturn to the natal Saturn approximately every few years. This varies by several factors, but as long as you know the day of your birth, you can look this up. It is not necessary to have the birth time. The book to consult is called an ephemeris, and is a collection of astrological information that says when a planet was in a particular sign at any given point, and is generally collected a century at a time, so it is more or less a once in a lifetime purchase. When transiting Saturn is two signs away from your natal Saturn, you are going through a Saturn sextile. What this means is that we find it is easier to learn lessons during those times. In context of this work, this time period also means it is a time that is personally easier for you to call on and work with Set. You may experience this is a period of above average manifestations.

Every time transiting Saturn enters into a sign that has the same element of the natal sign, you are experiencing a transit Saturn trining the natal one. What this means is that if you don't put any extra work into your personal workings having to do with Set, then life goes on, and things stay the same. However, if you decide to put in the effort, you may find that the work you do during that window builds a long lasting stable foundation for long term growth, the type of which has to do with your statement of intent from the working with Set. During these times it is also wise to do an extended ritual format rather than a one-time ritual. During the period of the transiting sextile, though, you may find is an excellent time for that. The results of the ritual done during the sextile will also have a tendency to manifest faster and easier than those that occur during the transiting trine. But, the results from the transiting trine will be of greater lasting value and foundation.

Now you can see where there is so much emphasis on the squares and oppositions of Saturn. If things are going well for us, then we are more likely to relax and go with the times. But when challenges arise, we want to know more to address the situation and in that way to move through it as fast as possible. It's the way the human brain is. We are naturally hardwired to focus on the negative. Humans are animals, after all, and as such, there are animalistic traits that are biological and instinctual. It is also clear that there is an ebb and flow to life, which we all know, but with this material it becomes clear what one of the causes is. This also makes the connection with Set clear, too.

Set

So much has been written about the Egyptian god Set that I am not going to attempt to be all-inclusive with this piece. Rather, I will highlight certain character traits that have to do with what we're discussing here. Originally, he was the god of the desert and storms. Later in development he became blended, along with Pan and other beings, into what would become the Judeo-Christian devil. This mingling took place over an extended period of time, and while that was happening his character was evolving. Eventually, he came to encompass all things malevolent and dark. Considering the fact that this was occurring at the beginning of the Age of Pisces, we can see how he would have also come to represent all things related to darker emotions and basically anything that doesn't make one feel good. The last two thousand years has been the Age of Pisces, meaning that a lot of the lessons the human species have been dealing with have to do with emotions and the healthy handling thereof. Another major area of focus during this time has been on religion, spirituality, occultism, and all things related to psychism. People generally feel better about themselves when their desires are satiated and gratification has been had.

Consequentially, as has been true as of late, there has been a lot of emphasis on youth. It is only now that we as a species are evolving past this emotionally immature yet spiritually potent time period, and will soon be entering the Age of Aquarius. That is a conversation for another time, though. We can now see that yes, Set and Saturn are therefore the devil, because they represent a lot of subjects that many people might not be emotionally comfortable exploring. This is even reflected in the fact that a title of Saturn is "The Greater Malefic." Set has been the riposte to the dominant paradigm for the last two thousand years, but as we move into the next age, which is Saturnine, his role will be evolving.

The sign Aquarius is co-ruled by Uranus and Saturn, and it is in this we see the role of Set will be increasing over approximately the next two thousand years. Astrologically speaking, Saturn is considered in a weak place when it is located in Pisces, and if we look at this as symbolic, what it tells us is that Set's power has been greatly diminished over the last two thousand years. Yes, diminished from its full potency which would have existed before the Age of Pisces. Since Saturn is seen as being strong when in Aquarius, we see that his power and potency is going to not only be stronger for approximately the next two thousand years, things will work out for the best in a gentler way than what has been the norm in this last age. In short, as much as we are coming into the Age of Aquarius, we are also entering into the first of two Saturn ages, for the Age of Capricorn follows Aquarius, and Saturn is the ruling planet there, too. This means we are about to enter into approximately four thousand years of Saturn and Set dominance.

This does put the onus on us, individually and collectively as a species, to emotionally step up and work through what we need to in order to welcome the incoming energies. We can do this by working with Set in his role of initiator. Regardless of what attribute of his you choose from the above list, each one is an initiation of sorts. Whether it is the initiation into full adulthood that comes with the first Saturn return, or a reminder that the only constant is change, which is a lesson of the seven year itch, our consciousness changes with each Saturn cycle we experience in our lives.

Praxis

What can we do with this information then? On one hand all of this can be useful for charting the rhythm in our lives, so in this way, this information can be of value even if we don't work with it magically. By knowing how lessons and cycles work, we can attune ourselves to the natural progression of life and thereby come to know ourselves better, which is the ultimate goal of spiritual ascent. On a more ritualistic note, though, we can see that there is great value to be found here if we take the time and do the work. Let's look at different ways we can apply this knowledge. The first thing to do is to figure out where Saturn is. You can use an ephemeris to discover this information, and when you do find it, the first thing to pay attention to above all else is the element that corresponds to Saturn. If it is in the element of earth, the lessons will have to do with the physical world and our interaction with it. If it is in the element of water, lessons having to do with emotions, spirituality, the occult, and psychism will be most pronounced. In the element of fire, the lessons will be action based, but will also include tests of will and resolve. In astrology, fire is also the divine spark that resides within each of us, so many of the lessons may also have to do with how strongly one feels connected with divinity. If Saturn is in an air element the lessons will be psychological and may have to do with learning new concepts and ways of thinking. These lessons may also have to do with personal relationships and social graces.

When it becomes clear what Saturn will have to do with during his cycles (he's known as a masculine planet that corresponds to earth), you can now proceed to address how you are going to incorporate Set into these time periods. For example, if you know your next Saturn cycle that is coming up is going to be in the element of water, you can work with Set to teach you the emotional, psychic, and empathetic lessons that are needed for your greatest growth and good. If the element is earth, then perhaps working with Set in a more tangible way would be wiser. I'm sure at this point you see what I'm saying. It is in this way we tap into the idea that Set goes out in front of Ra's solar barque and clears his passage through the Duat. In this instance we work him to clear the path for our spiritual growth and path forward. I am reminded here of the correspondence of his that says he strips away in order to purify. Much like being in the desert sun for an extended period of time, we can purify ourselves by working with him to clear our path ahead.

Another way we can use this information is retroactively. Armed with this material, we can reflect on lessons that have been brought to us from previous times in our lives and see what we gleaned from them through new eyes, as it were. This is particularly useful because it allows us to forecast, in a broad sense, what may be coming down the road as far as tests and initiations are concerned. If we can look back at situations in our lives and see the lesson, we can then see if we passed the test or not, and if we didn't, we can now have an idea of how it will manifest when it comes back around, if we didn't pass it. If we did pass it, though, it would be good to keep our eyes open for opportunities that have to do with those lessons that are brought to our door for us to demonstrate what we have learned from the previous time.

By incorporating this material to whatever degree you feel comfortable with, you put yourself in a position to become proactive when it comes to taking charge of your life and in particular your spiritual growth and personal development. Knowing these Saturn cycles will at least tell you what's coming and give you a tool for assessment for your life lessons. On the magical end of the spectrum, this underscores the reason to work with Set. Yes, this also means you could apply this line of thinking to other beings that correspond to Saturn. This opens the door to work with Saturn in ways that are in line with your own spiritual paradigm. While I personally prefer Set, you could adapt this material to Satan, Pan, or any other Saturn correspondent being. In this way we also see the universal archetype that Set represents: initiation, impermanency, and fatality, but all as part of the natural processes of life. He is a reminder of the wisdom of the American poet, Jim Morrison: "No one here gets out alive."

BAPTIZED IN THE ECSTASY OF POISON

Cătălina Deaconu

In the sameness of the Great Desert of Set it is easy to get lost. There's no map, there's only you. Looking up to the sky, the sun can be seen projecting all its light upon you - it feels like the whole of your life essence is being pushed out from your body, and a scent of rotting flesh intoxicates your senses. Have you become a walking corpse? The distorted image of your palms, your legs heavy as lead and your mind shattered beyond repair, they all tell you to let go, to fall down onto your fiery deathbed.

You close your eyes, waiting for the eternal slumber. You've lost all ties with reality and the only thing that is keeping you alive is purely your own will. You cannot allow yourself to die. Your throat is dried up, the sound of your own dying screech terrifies your very being. You're not afraid of death, just terribly angry that you didn't finish your appointed mission. In a moment of unexplained ecstasy, you give your last straw, wholly liberating the fury of your innermost Dragon in a raging powerful scream. That's how you mark the hour of your death, the climax of the Evil Day, the moment of your deepest pain releasing a powerful psychic blast which creates an entire world.

You are now the Creator, and the Desert is given to you.

Such is the nature of Set. He is the enemy of boundaries and defies death itself. He shows us that there is always a choice and that you can extract strength from everything, even when we think that there are no chances left.

The origin of his name is still uncertain by modern etymological standards, but I think that we should take in consideration some of the following interpretations. Plutarch's take on it is that the name of Set can possibly mean "the overmastering," "overpowering," but can also mean "overpassing" and "turning back."

Let's take a closer look at this, and what "overpowering" can reveal. We can bring about for analysis another ancient god, this one from Persia. The legend of Mithra (1) has him jumping on top of the bull that attacks him, instead of fighting it, and riding the bull until it's exhausted of all its power, to only then slay it with his sword. The bull here represents the world itself, as Taurus' astral nature makes it a common representation of the cosmos, showing then how we don't need to sabotage ourselves by surrendering to the natural laws. Fate is in our own hands. You can embrace fury, your lust for power and your most antinomian passions which torment you from the inside. That's how we free ourselves from their influences, by accepting that they are a part of our Self, and riding their wave like Mithra rides the bull. The word of sin is restriction, which is always a good thing to keep in mind. "Turning back," on its turn, accentuates the adversarial spirit of Set, putting in perspective the concept of reversal, or inversion, of energies deeply connected with subjects such as Kundalini, which requires the inversion of the polarities of Ida and Pingala before they can be synthesized in the Sushumna, and the Black Sun, or Sol Inversus, as well as the theory of the Qliphoth being the anti-structure of the Sephiroth, the entropy consequential of any expansive motion. The Left Hand Path is antinomian in essence, and an initiate on the Path of the Dragon never submits to the natural, or any other, order. We can also interpret this as turning back to Nothingness, the Womb of the Dragon. Last but not least, it can be associated with the act of abandonment in times of need, showing once again that he is not bound by trivial human conventions, devoid of obligations to others and capable of letting go of what is futile, by "turning his back." Another concept of potential interest is brought about by M.A. Murray, suggesting the name of Set as meaning "to intoxicate, to cause to be drunken," which takes us to the cult of Bacchus. By intoxicating yourself, you make yourself vulnerable, making room for the Dark Gods to rip apart the impurities of the mundane world from your mind, body and soul. It also denotes the abortive character of Set, with alcohol consumption being a great danger to human pregnancy, a subject that will be approached later in this essay.

Concerning the many legends surrounding Set, some of you may have heard about the Ennead of Heliopolis. In the beginning was Atum, the Absolute, the Lord of All, and by means of self-fecundation he created one pair of gods, male and female: Shu and Tefnut, from which the concept of duality arose into the world. From the sexual union between Shu and Tefnut, the god Geb and the goddess Nut came into being, who later brought forth Osiris and Isis. Up to that point, things were in absolute harmony, each pair producing only one set of male and female twins. Then a twist of sorts arrived, because it wasn't just Osiris and Isis to come into being on their generation, but also Set and Nephthys. Thus, the birthday of Set is the beginning of confusion and subversion, even before his name existed. He is not bound to natural laws, his birth ignites the desire to transcend and pervert duality, which from my perspective plays a huge part in awakening the Black Flame within. He despises order and spits on those who submit to the natural course of events, unwilling to break the veil covering their eyes and see beyond a limited perception. The same can be said about the desert, as when everything looks alike and no escape is naturally offered, you have to lift yourself above everything and carve your own unique path. Set is, then, unpredictable, violently letting his fury drive him rather than suppressing it.

He is also untimely born. Plutarch tells us: "not in due season or manner, but with a blow he broke through his mother's side and leapt forth," which proclaims him as a self-created god. In the Egyptian Book of the Dead, Papyrus of Ani, we have Tem-Khephera's statement "I have created myself with Nu, in the name of Khephera." Nu embodies Nothingness in its purest and rawest form, the clean night sky, while Tem-Khephera is the god who created all the other ones, including himself. We learn from Kenneth Grant that "It is futile and false to imagine a coin with one side only," so we may easily draw a parallel between Khephera and see Set as the dark side of that coin, as he takes over the creative force of nature and enforces his destructive will upon it. Pyramid texts go as far as completely avoiding the verb "to be born" whenever the name of Set is mentioned.

There is also the story of Anat and Astarte, goddesses also worshipped in Egypt, who couldn't bear their pregnancy to an end. It is said that their wombs were closed by Horus, but then opened by Set, causing them to abort the fetus. This made Set feared in the hearts of pregnant women, who, in the Greek period wore amulets with inscriptions such as "Contract womb, lest Typhon seize upon you." Just like Lilith, the Mother of Abortions, he challenges the initiate to find objective immortality within, instead of the subjective immortality of perpetuating the species, akin to Tantra and the Devayana, the notion of spiritually reproducing with the gods instead of for the flesh. (2)

In the Turin papyrus, Set can be found saying, "I am a Man of a million cubits, whose name is Evil Day. As for the day of giving birth or of conceiving, there is no giving birth and trees bear no fruits." Here, we could be surprised by Set identifying with the word "Man," but simple as this may sound, the meaning behind it is without a doubt fascinating. This can be likened to a phrase such as Crowley's "There is no God, but Man," in Liber OZ. I like to think that it could be nice for us to not fuss as much trying to be like gods and perhaps focus on simply being, because the truth is that we are already gods in the flesh. Everything we can potentially have is within us, and the roar of the Dragon waits to be liberated so it can expand beyond what we usually think we are capable of. The blood of the Dragon is bursting in our veins. It is just a matter of choice if we allow ourselves to harness its limitless power or let it be wasted in vain. That's not the same as saying we should disregard or disrespect the Draconian Gods. On the contrary, we should be more than grateful that we have them on our side. But in the end, we aren't bound to them and we have to realize that we are our own gods. By learning their lessons and assimilating their qualities, we become aware of the inner treasure that is deeply buried within us, and only through ceaseless effort, after burning the midnight oil and sorting out the best ideas and solutions for an unexpected yet so fervently desired breakthrough, we bring it to the surface, with the realization that everything that is without is also always within. Thus, the Serpent's promise is being ultimately fulfilled when we claim our freedom and conquer that sacred moment of pure bliss which lasts forever, hovers us inside out, all being attained by the force of our will and a constant perfecting of the Self. He is "a Man of a million cubits" because his nature is infinite. He is called "evil" to conceal his holiness.

He is the Adversary whose day marks the end and the beginning of all. When you gaze into eternity, fruits don't grow anymore because you're above the need for them. You are now the Creator and the Destroyer because Set shows those acts are one and the same. All this reveals how Set cannot but be hated by the mindless ignorance of those still enslaved, who are bound to the material world, lacking any desire for transcendence. For that very reason he can be a defining inspirational model and ultimate guiding force for those who walk the daring Path of the Dragon.

As for the conflict between Horus and Set, it is perhaps too wide to be covered in a few lines. In some legends, Set lost his testicles and Horus lost his eye during their battle. It is not uncommon to perceive the Eye of Horus as a separate entity, but if we take a closer look at a relevant section of the Berlin Papyrus (4), it says: "I pull out the finger of Set from the eye of Horus" (3), and by this identification between one's eye and the other's finger, the meaning becomes clear. The phallus and the finger are often associated in Western and Eastern culture with solar phallic deities that are usually presented raising a finger, i.e. ithyphalically. By the solar power of Set, he lights up the Eye of Horus, giving it life. Thus, we may say that without Set the Eye of Horus wouldn't be, either. He is the one who gives a purpose to his enemy, because he is All and not even his enemies can define him, the opposition being instrumental but not essential for the "Man of a million cubits" who transcends duality and opposition, perceiving the enemy as a part of himself. Thus, he grows bigger than enmity itself. Horus is the embodiment of Light, the life giver, Set is also the one who extinguishes the life force from Horus' Eye and here we see him as the one who drops the curtain, letting us pierce into the Void and showing us that "Being itself cannot be without reference to Non-Being," realizing that the world as we know it not only arose from Nothingness but ultimately still is inherently Nothingness.

Not much is said, unfortunately, about the testicles of Set, but we should take into consideration the alchemical adage "In Cauda Semper Stat Venenum" (The poison can always be found in the tail), and the tail suggests a phallic symbol, the pronounced extremity, which is also the tail of the Dragon. His poison is the "seed of the scorpion." Thus, Set's semen and poison are interchangeable. Here we are dealing with a set of opposites, semen being a masculine element and poison being a feminine element (menstruum). This grows interesting as we inspect Aleister Crowley mentioning that the Setian nature is to be read in any divine names with the letters S and T to their names (4), even in Saturn, so we can safely look into other traditions for answers about those letters without fearing too much we may run out of Set's scope, especially as we don't have much historically accurate information on Egyptian sacred correspondences for letters.

The "S" seems very straightforward, accentuating his serpentine force, the inner Dragon, the Kundalini, the fire within, and many more relevant correspondences, just by pairing it up with the Kabbalistic notion of the Hebrew Shin. Those are all symbols we should be used to by now. The "T," however, may invite some deeper esoteric and symbolic scrutiny. The Kabbalah presents the Hebrew Taw as representing synthesis and man, again relevant. Perhaps the most telling meaning is to be found in the Greek letter Tau, as well as the Gnostic ideas attributed to both the letter and the symbol. They regarded it as the Spiritual Seal of Man that gave us the right to exercise Divine Will on Earth, allowing us to step from lower magic to higher magic, i.e. Theurgy. Going back to Crowley, he puts this very sign on the Magus' forehead (5), and notes that it isn't a regular T in that case, but an upward T with the vertical line pointing up. Seeing it that way, the very graphic symbol clearly denotes a phallic expression. The feminine power of the Dragon, in the Shin, is thus united with the masculine power of the phallus, marking the beginning and the end of Set's name. The turning of the "T" upward can also be associated with the inverted motion of Kundalini and directing the sexual power upward instead of downward and into the world as it would flow in its natural state, that of profane love and reproduction. With the aid of sexual magick, then, we can see the female and the male becoming one, the duality transcended and the notion of time disappearing, leaving with any sense of incompletion or lack, and destroying the roots of all powerlessness.

With this arcanum in mind, the hint Grant gives us, quoting "Man" as the Lost Word in Illuminati Initiation and suggesting this as an essential stage on the Magic Revival the book is named after, reveals its Kabbalistic nature, because Adam Kadmon, the Perfect Man who held full divine power, had his woman, the female principle, inside of himself (6), in perfect union, and by becoming aware of this fact and working to achieve it by any means necessary we fulfill the Serpent's promise. The Lost Word is the Womb and the Grave, the Beginning and the End, on the highest of heavens and in the lowest of hells, all being the same, just like shown by the nature of the Ouroboros.

Then having analyzed all these mechanisms of Typhonian interplay and noticed that the gear keeping them all in motion is none other than True Will, an even deeper connection can be found with Aleister Crowley's definition of it by: "True Will should spring, a fountain of Light, from within, and flow unchecked, seething with Love into the Ocean of Life." A sentiment also echoes in a poem that whispers truth into the Void, A Poison Tree by William Blake, where True Will appears as not having oppositions or enemies because it shatters everything that stands in its way. It is fiery, wrathful and full of lust, lust being the desire born out of desire itself without any kind of attachments. When loss becomes strength, lust becomes the "enemy of boundaries," just like Set, and deeply related to the Beast, as it is depicted in the Lust card in the Thoth deck. And the Beast itself warns us to follow Set closely when it declares in Revelation 3:16: "But since you are neither hot nor cold, but only lukewarm, I will spit you out of my mouth." Set is a being of extremities and excesses, never satisfied, just like Lust. The hot and the cold cannot be bound, but lukewarm is the moderate way of the faint-hearted ones who get stuck in the middle and never progress, endlessly trying to move forward without success. By walking the Left Hand Path and embracing the extremes like Set, in order to become the masters of our own destiny, we do not leave the insides of the Beast. Echoing Set, who didn't accept to be spat from his mother's womb, we don't accept to be spat from the Beast's mouth and we ride it fearlessly to the end of the Apocalypse. That's one of the most precious advices that Set leaves us with, but there are many, many more, and the decision to listen and put them into application is up to us.

He is a being more ancient than mankind and it is impossible to cover his nature in just one essay. That is why it is always necessary to keep looking, doing studies of your own and bringing forth your unique revelations. Once you walk the Path of the Dragon, many doors will open. It depends solely on you if you'll find the courage to burst into them or be blinded by your mindless ignorance and step away from these never-ending opportunities.

FOOTNOTES:

(1) Franz Cumont: *The Mysteries of Mithra.*
(2) Julius Evola: *Metaphysics of Sex.*
(3) cit. p.H. Te Velde, Seth, God of Confusion.
(4) Aleister Crowley: *Book of Thoth.*
(5) ibid., '2. The Lord of Illusion'.
(6) Genesis 1:27. says "Male and female created them" on the inception of Adam, long before Eve is ever mentioned, and

the Book of Enoch presents the creation of Eve as already a kind of Fall from Grace, because it divided Adam's absolute powers.

THE GIFT OF DEMISE

Mimi Hazim

Enter Sutekh, the God of chaos and storm,
He draws the blade and across my soul does score,
a map of shadow, of transmutation.
I feel the steel slash against my etheric body,
My abdomen shakes, my pelvis shatters.

In spite of the pain, I do not beg, I do not scream.
I open myself to the onslaught; hurt me more.

As I lay spent upon the crimson desert sands,
the storm clouds pass overhead to reveal Ra in all of his
glory.
My dismembered flesh burns under his searing weight and
guise.
The vulture pecks at my glazed eyes as the desert viper
gracefully passes me by, seeking cool sanctuary as refuge
from the heat.

As the hours pass, the sun soon sets, and night provides a
cooling blanket to my worn and ravaged corpse.

*Only the stars above may hold testament of what remains
of me, and my material form.*

*As for Sutekh, he is not done with me yet.
With just a breath, the cracks of my body begin to shine
and gleam,
as my congealed blood takes on an ophidian sheen,
transforming into a most glorious gold.*

*As my reparations gather swift momentum, he speaks life
into me once more,
and I am reborn anew within his gaze,
as I hear his voice upon the wind, of a quality known to no
terrestrial ear.*

*I offer gratitude to my captor, my destroyer, my father, my
saviour.
I am whole again.*

WALKING WITH SET

Keona Kai'Nathera

I started out on a 30-day working with Set, to do a ritual or meditation or something every day to be able to contribute to this anthology. But, that did not happen. Instead, he led me through what I needed to experience in my time with him. Neither did we work together the whole 30 days. In the beginning I was really upset, thinking that I failed and did not do what I sat out to do. Then I realized that nothing planned works the way you want. It works the way it is needed. Below is how my working with Set began.

In anticipation of the book of Set coming out, I decided to reach out to my beloved Father as it is. I have never purposefully worked with him. It has always been him there when it was needed or warranted. But, I had another reason to reach out. I wanted to include him in a large scale working that I have been working on for a few years now, and wanted and needed his guidance and approval to move forward. To do so, I had to really get to know him. There was material and research I had on him, but I planned on expounding what wasn't there so I could be more personal with him. What I planned on doing was having a closer relationship with Set. He being God of Storms, and married to Nebet-het, who I connect with, was just a reason to really reach out and connect.

I decided to jump all in, and what happens, happens. I still believe that being completely open and just allowing natural progress is the perfect way to be exposed to his energy and influence. I purchased a small statue that I can look upon and touch during ascensions, prayers and meditations to Set.

With Set I worked with Mars, fire, and projective energy. There is a lot of information that I had, but decided to do what felt natural, instead of just making something happen. In the connection with him, I did receive a personal sigil which I remember from a few years ago, although I had no contact or thought of him in my mind back then.

I did ask him if he wanted a blood offering, he grabbed my hand and said "No, just come and see me."

The second day with him I asked if he would like a blood offering. He paused, looked at me, studying me, and said "no." He again said come and see him. At this time, I was holding his statue in my left hand and running my thumb along the side of his statue.

I decided to have my own correspondences to him based on the energy and vibes I was getting from him, the scents I smelled, and trusting my eyes in what he was showing me. I felt that working with him during the Dark Moon would be more suitable for him. Also, planetary workings with Saturn, Mars and Pluto (my added choice) felt natural. Because of who he is, these planets were more organic for my personal connection to him. I also wanted to explore these 72 generals of Set, which I have my own theory about, but not going to share here.

We talked late into the night, early in the morning. He called me his Daughter, and said just because I didn't come from him doesn't make me less a part of his family or a part of his blood. He said we all come from Mother. I asked him, is it because my significant other is his son that he has always been aware of me? He smiled and nodded, and said he always watches his children's mates. It isn't a lot of their mates that have ambitions that catch his eye, so when he does take an interest, it is intense. I then asked him if he would work with me and he said he will guide me in my blood workings. He seemed intrigued with my idea. He gave me a sigil, very simplistic in design.

Being a curious creature, and bold one at that, I reached out and touched his face. I just wanted to cry. So smooth, so warm. His hair was thick and long, straight but a little wavy. It was deep blood red, like crimson. He had freckles on his dark skin. He was, of course, way taller than normal, what we would typically think of as being a god height. He was wearing a red sash around his waist, and a kilt like garment underneath it. He was of muscular build, a bluish tinge to his deep mahogany skin. His left bicep had a tattoo wrapped around it. It was too dark for me to decipher it, but it looked like a mural of some types of animals I haven't seen before. He said it was 9 with 8, and then sort of smiled.

On day 5, I carried his statue with me to work. I saw him slightly differently, with rich dark brown skin, tinged red. He had dark red hair, red slits of eyes and freckles. His ears were cute, reminding me of Anpu's. He had a long nose, but it seemed to ebb and flow. I saw Set more as a human male, than a humanoid. He had a calm demeanor on this day, but he was twitching like he was ready to be on the move, but still encouraged to take my time and connect with him. We were just sitting on the sand dunes, feeling the warm breeze dance around us. I heard sounds but couldn't seem to identify any of them. The sun was high, but it was not very hot. It was warm and gentle - the essence of being sun kissed. His clothes were flopping around him, the colorful sash around his waist, the cloth over his chest moved in waves as if the fabric was made of water. I saw the mysterious tattoo that seemed to go from his left bicep over his chest and on to his other arm. His face was constantly morphing and changing with the breeze, like he was wanting to experience every bit of the wind, ears moving as if listening to the whispers in the wind, or perhaps my thoughts. I wanted to breathe in the chaos, destruction, protection and healing that emanated off of him. The Dark Moon was getting closer, he reminded me.

Set's mini statue is extremely intense. I stare at it. I feel strength, determination and confidence. It is a self-awareness I am not quite familiar. His mouth is in a tight curve like his nose, giving him the appearance of Wile E. Coyote from Looney Tunes of my youth. With his statue, I see him staring across the desert, his domain. He is teaching me ways to be close to the earth, to be one and to form with the sands, to control and wield the power that it unleashes.

On day 7 my time with him was really good. Gentle, even. I felt that this is the way I am supposed to get to know him. Personally. At my own pace, at his own pace. To be completely free and open to him with no expectations of what I *wanted* to do.

Seeing as Set

Invoking him was very cool to say the least. First of all, my mouth had a mind of its own. I decided that I would invoke Set at work! I paid for that, but it was a learning experience, and the only thing bruised was my coworkers' egos. I wanted to see what he saw, and have him see what I see. Well, that went sideways and he decided he wanted to work a part of my shift. He had me being a little more forceful, and since I work in the medical field; every once in a while, we need to tell the person on the phone (always a coworker) to shut up and actually listen to what I am saying. I felt a lot more confident than I had in the past working with them and he made sure that I let myself be heard, and that I could control the chaos that they were throwing at me, and turn it into what I needed to stay sane.

After a couple of hours, I was able to get the staff under control and minimize my phone calls. As I was driving home it literally rained hard as hell in a few certain sections of the highway and as I got closer to home. Of course, when I asked him a question or make a comment, it started to rain very hard, and I distinctively heard deep laughter every time. It stopped as I pulled up to my house. Just when I opened the gate, I felt a deep rumble from within me and then it was a torrential pour for 5 minutes and he just laughed.

I swear these Gods have a sense of humor.

I made it thirteen days into my 30-day ritual work. And to be honest, those thirteen days was just what I needed. For the rest of the month, I just focused on his statue and his presence and I was calm, more forceful and able to take some of the worst situations and bring them to order. I always saw him as Chaos and Destruction, but my time with him was full of laughter, vivid imagery, reflection, and a peace I had not felt before.

THE LORD OF FIRE

Asenath Mason

This working is centered on the Lord of Fire as an archetype of the inner power, or the inner evolutionary force. This force can be referred to as the Black Flame of Set, the Ascending Flame of Lucifer, the Promethean Fire, and so on. There are many god-forms that can be used to embody this concept. In this ritual, we will work with three god-forms representing the archetype of the inner fire:

- Set as the lord of the inner flame/inner power/center of the fire within
- Lucifer as the lord of the ascending flame/the fire in movement
- Azazel as the lord of transformation through fire/the master of inner alchemy

Why these three god-forms?

Set is connected with the archetype of fire in many ways. He is the god of the desert, representing the scorching rays of the sun. Hence he is a "red god" - the red color referring to his fiery nature as well as to the desert, the crimson blaze of the sun, desert storms, the burning heat, and his red hair with which he is often depicted in art. The Desert of Set in the Typhonian Tradition is the Crimson Desert of Daath, associated with the Qabalistic Abyss, the place of desolation and nothingness. Again, we encounter here the connection to the red color, which is also symbolic of fire. The sun in ancient Egypt was viewed as a deadly force because it burned the land and dried the crops, causing death and famine. His fiery nature can also be interpreted as sexual energy as fire is also a symbol of lust, passion, desire, and sex drive. This aspect of Set is also relevant to this ritual as we will work with fire in its dynamic, creative form. In this respect, he is sometimes associated with Sekhmet, the fierce lion goddess whose fiery nature is often interpreted in terms of sexual heat as well. The symbol of both of them is the letter *Sh,* or in the Draconian/Typhonian Tradition, the letter *Shin*, which is the letter typifying fire, the spirit, and the Fire Snake/Kundalini - the driving force behind all creation and all evolution. Apart from that, Set is also associated with Typhon, the fire-breathing dragon representing the force of volcanoes - hence another connection with fire. Set is therefore the Lord of Fire, or more specifically, the Inner Flame, and in this aspect we will refer to him in this ritual.

Lucifer as the Lord of the Ascending Flame represents the force in movement. The Ascending Flame is a symbol that can be interpreted in many ways. It can be seen as a human desire of transcendence - the inner drive that compels us to become something better: a higher form of consciousness, an advanced spiritual being, or simply a better person. This desire is in all of us. It can manifest in positive ways, driving us to growth and evolution, or negatively - when we are consumed by our own desires or controlled by our urges instead of controlling them. Again, this is connected to the idea of Kundalini - the force that can be as liberating as enslaving. The ascent of the Fire Snake dissolves consciousness in a "death-like" experience, which can lead either to ecstasy and bliss or to madness and death if we lack the discipline of concentration and persistence in the work. Lucifer is the Lord of Flames, but also the Light Bearer - and thus he represents not only the force of ascent and evolution but also illumination and enlightenment. While the flame of Set is believed to be black, Lucifer's fire is golden - connecting the celestial realms with the underworld, or heaven and hell - if we look at the legend of his descent from the heights to the depths. He is both a luminous angelic being and a lord of darkness. His light, however, is fiery - it is the fire of the Adversary, the inner flame, the divine radiance within. This is the Ascending Flame - the force we will work with in this ritual.

Finally, there is Azazel, another "Lord of Fire." If you are not familiar with his mythology, let me say a few words about it. According to the Books of Enoch, Azazel was the leader of the angels that descended from heaven to marry the daughters of man. Some sources mention Shemyaza as the leader, and others present these two as one and the same figure. The angels not only rebelled against God and the divine laws by having sexual contacts with mortal women but also brought down divine knowledge to the earth, like Prometheus bringing down the divine fire from the heights. This knowledge included the art of warfare, alchemy, witchcraft, the art of make-up, the knowledge of precious stones, coloring substances, and metals of the earth. Azazel's gift was alchemy, the art and science of transformation, which refers both to the transmutation of metals and to the art of forging and perfecting the spirit/soul. He is therefore another archetype of an initiator of mankind, the Adversary leading man on the way to self-deification. The key terms in the symbolism of Azazel are thus awakening and transgression. His gift to humanity is the divine fire that is the essence of angels and entities that dwell in the higher dimensions - the force behind all growth and evolution. Before he descended to the earth, he was one of the

Seraphim, the burning ones. An interesting thing to note is that apart from being creatures of fire, the Seraphim were also described as winged serpents or dragons - hence another connection to the concept of the Fire Snake. The gift of Azazel is therefore inner alchemy, the art of transforming the divine spark within into the fiery pillar of ascent - the knowledge of transmutation of man from the creature of clay to a god-like being.

Fire itself is a symbol that offers many interpretations - in both positive and negative sense. It stands for change, willpower, creativity, motivation, dynamic energy, force in movement, etc. It is creative and destructive, warming and scorching, life-giving and consuming everything, protection and weapon. It burns and purifies. It is also sexuality and passion, both physical and spiritual. Other symbols associated with it are the red color, the south in ritual systems, the summer as a time of the year, etc. We can find many associations and interpretations if only we look around. In rituals we use fire for purification, healing, burning the cords, destroying attachments, and many other forms of magic. It provides a point of connection between the worlds, representing the center - which is also one of the symbolic meanings of the Black Flame of Set or the Golden Flame of Lucifer. It is both a beginning and a completion. By invoking fire we become consumed, transformed and liberated from our limitations. It is also a symbol of authority, leadership, and strength - the breath of the Dragon, the vehicle of ascent, and the emblem of power.

The following working activates and raises the Serpent Force/Kundalini and directs its flow in a way that is a little bit different from how it is usually worked with. For this purpose we will use two symbols: the trident and the ankh.

The trident is connected with fire in many ways. It stands for the letter Shin and represents the pillar of ascent on the path of the Draconian Initiation. In our work, it can be related to Lucifer and serves as a key to his current. It can also represent Azazel, because the trident is one of the weapons forged in his living fire through his rites of transformation and inner alchemy. Finally, it is also connected with Set, as one of the meanings of the god's name is "a standing stone" or "pillar." In Draconian Tradition and Luciferian Gnosis we can view the trident as symbolic of three channels, or nadis, through which the Fire Snake flows through the subtle body of man: Ida (the left nadi), Pingala (the right nadi), and Shushumna (the central nadi) equivalent to the spinal cord. This corresponds to the mystical meaning of the number 3, forming the concept of three in one. This meaning is a subject for another time, though. Suffice to say, it is the number of the holy or unholy trinity, but it is also symbolic of man as a point of connection and the intermediary between the above and below, heaven and hell, the inner and the outer. We will use this paradigm to work with the energy flow in the following ritual, assuming the trident position in meditation and visualizing three flames rising through the three main nadis to form one flame. The trident position means that you have to stand straight with your arms raised so that your body forms the shape of the trident, making yourself a living vessel for the energies of the Draconian Current to flow through, or in other words, transforming yourself into the Lord of Fire.

The ankh is a widely recognized symbol as well, known as the key of life or crux ansata (the cross with a handle). One of its foremost meanings is eternal life, and in ancient Egyptian art gods are often portrayed bearing one in each hand or carrying it by its loop, usually with arms crossed over their chest. Another common depiction of this symbol is in the scenes where the pharaoh is offered the ankh by the gods as a blessing and bestowal of eternal life. In this interpretation, the vertical section below the crossbar can be viewed as a symbol of the path on the earth, or the mundane life that is short and temporary, while the loop stands for the eternal life that has no beginning or end. We can therefore view it as a key to the mystery of life, death, and resurrection in the afterlife. However, if we look at it from the perspective of the inner alchemy, we can also see it as symbolic of the flow of energy within the body. Here we come to the purpose of this ritual.

There is a Kundalini-raising technique that uses the ankh as a symbol for directing the inner energy to flow through specific chakras. This technique revitalizes health, rejuvenates the body, and improves the circulation of inner energy. It is called "ankhing," or "Egyptian Tantra," and it is usually focused on sexual energy that is released through orgasm. How does it work? It combines several techniques to work with the flow of Kundalini - i.e. deep breathing, visualization, and sex trance. In our ritual, we will work with it in a different way, but feel free to experiment with it on your own by using the sex trance technique and the physical orgasm. The visualization starts with the root chakra (Muladhara) at the base of the spine - the seat of the Fire Snake. Then the flow of energy is directed to the heart chakra or to the throat - there are several variations of this technique. At this point the energy is visualized in the shape of an arch or a loop and directed to the crown chakra on top of the head, and then back to the heart. The flow of energy resembles then the Egyptian ankh. If the center of the meditation is the heart chakra, the energy in a natural way connects to the universe, thus completing the flow and forming the full ankh.

In the following ritual we will combine both techniques. In the first part of the meditation we will assume the trident position, placing ourselves in the center of the universe and connecting to the worlds above and below. Then we will direct the flow of the Fire Snake to form the ankh shape and to balance the circuit. To awaken and activate the Fire Snake we will use a technique called "the breath of fire." You can also use the physical orgasm, but in my own practice I have found the breath of fire technique more effective in this work. Feel free to experiment with it, though.

In this work we will activate and direct the flow of the inner fire so that it may be used as a vehicle of evolution and the force of transcendence. This energy can be experienced in many ways - you can feel it as a vital force, strengthening your body, cleansing your chakras, and improving your health. It can also be felt in a sexual way, releasing intense emotions, from love and passion to anger and fury. It is creative because it can be used to push your intent toward manifestation, but it can also be destructive - used to burn your enemies, your harmful habits, obstacles on your path, etc.

The first part of the meditation will fill you with living fire - if you perform it properly, you should literally feel as if you were burning. The breath of fire technique will also raise your blood pressure and increase your heartbeat, therefore be careful with it if you suffer from any heart or respiratory issues. In this case, my advice is to simply focus on breathing deeply and raising the Fire Snake in a steady rhythm. The ankh meditation, on the other hand, will bring your inner energy back in balance, providing a harmonious and steady flow. Combined together these methods form a powerful Kundalini-raising technique that can be used as a working in its own right or as a preliminary exercise before another ritual.

The flow of energy through the chakras

The Ritual

Everyone stands in the circle. For a while each participant focuses on the breathing cycle, taking a few deep breaths to relax and clear the mind.

The ritual begins by opening the gates to the Draconian Current and invocation of the inner Dragon/Serpent Force. All participants vibrate together the word **"VOVIN"** eleven times, building the atmosphere in the temple and creating the circuit of energy. Then the leader faces the altar, anoints the ritual blade with one's blood and draws the trident in the air, while reciting the following invocation:

By the power of my blood, the Blood of the Dragon,
And with the flaming trident which is the key to the gates
of the night,
I invoke the Lord of Fire,
Set-Lucifer-Azazel!
From the temple of light and darkness
I call to you, Master of the Living Flame,
Revealer of secrets and knowledge of the ancients,
Initiator of those who walk the Path of the Dragon!
Awaken the Serpent!
Open my eyes and show me what I need to see,
Open my ears and let me hear your voice from within,
Open my heart and transform it into living fire!

Set, Lord of the Inner Flame, ignite my will and make it
strong!
Lucifer, Lord of the Ascent, raise me from the mortal flesh
And let me ride your flaming breath to the heights of
heaven and the depths of hell!
Azazel, Lord of Transformation, change me as I walk
through the flames!

I call upon your life-giving and death-bringing essence!
Guide me to the truth,
Lead me to the core of my own power,
Let me burn and rise like a phoenix from the ashes,
And fill me with your living radiance
As I become one with you, and you become one with me.
May the fire within shine forth!

Everyone chants the following words for a while, in increasing volume, to build up the power in the temple and in the individual participants:

Set-Lucifer-Azazel

The leader stops the chants by exclaiming:

In Nomine Draconis!
Ho Drakon Ho Megas!

Then the leader guides the participants into an inner fire meditation. Of course, you can also do the ritual alone. It starts with activating "the breath of fire" - this is a strong and quick breath done from the navel point, which energizes and ignites the fire of life. Pull in the navel while exhaling through the nose. Then inhale and release the belly. Slowly increase the pace until breathing 2-3 times per second in and out through the nose. Continue for a few minutes. The leader can give the pace for the breathing rhythm by using a drum or another instrument.

At one point you will feel a stream of fire flowing through your spine and spreading all over your body. When this happens, raise your arms and stand in the trident position. You can still breathe with the breath of fire, but if it is too overwhelming, simply focus on the trident posture. Feel the fire going up through the palms of your hands and through the crown of your head - forming three flames rising above, connecting you to the worlds above. Then lower your arms, taking the current down, and feel how it flows from above to the soles of your feet and down, deep into the earth, connecting you with the realms below. You are now the axis of the world and the center of the universe - the pillar of living fire.

Then cross your arms on the chest, visualizing that all this energy flows into you and forms the shape of an ankh. It flows from your root chakra - focus on it and inhale a deep breath, visualizing a stream of fiery energy rising from the base of the spine to your heart chakra. Then hold your breath and focus on your heart. Visualize that the energy leaves your heart chakra out through your back, loops backward and flows up to the crown of your head. Focus on this energy center for a moment and then, still holding your breath, visualize that the fiery stream loops forward from your crown chakra down and back into your heart. Then exhale and direct the energy back to your root chakra. Keep doing this for a while, breathing slowly and deeply and holding your breath while visualizing the flow of energy. When you finish the meditation, lower your arms to your sides. You can also take some time for a personal communion with the Lord of Fire, e.g. asking him to burn the obstacles on your path or simply apply this force to a manifestation of a certain goal in your life.

The leader speaks:

I am the Secret Serpent coiled about to spring: in my coiling there is joy.
If I lift up my head, I and my Nuit are one.
If I droop down mine head, and shoot forth venom, then is rapture of the earth,
And I and the earth are one.

All participants drink the sacrament (wine, water, etc.)
while speaking the following words:

I am the Living Flame, the Serpent, and the Dragon.
Ho Ophis Ho Archaios,
Ho Drakon Ho Megas.

Close with the traditional words:

And so it is done!

RISING UP IN THE MIDDLE OF THE SANDSTORM

V. Ghallego-Iglesias

Whenever we look into a god, or any sacred symbols, we are not just studying and theoretically preparing for magical work. We are instead, at that very moment, performing a magical act. It consists of focusing our attention on a center of energy, on an aspect of the Logos, and then opening ourselves to receive its influences, using our will, our attention, and opening our very souls in that direction - and that is the main function of the soul - to be influenced and reshaped directly by everything that enters it through our senses and experiences, as it is there to embody the cosmos as the vastest mirror of all. We are filled at the same time by the desire to learn, to come, to transcend, as knowledge means nothing but possibility for transformation. Both that opening and the yearning desire for change, transformation and growth involved in this process, are an essential and definitely overlooked ingredient for any magical operation.

It is no exaggeration to even say this fulminant desire is magic itself, the hunger of the Dragon, the lust of a divine womb.

While this direct impulse toward mystery and transformation represented by learning is already an analogical image of magic itself, perhaps no other god could make that comparison as close and urgent, as eloquent and overt, as when we turn our attention to Set. He was already thought of originally as a creature of pure and absolute mystery and transformation before millennia, and this constant fascination has kept people reaching out for him over thousands of years. Each cycle of time adds new layers to his complexity, rendering his enigmatic nature even more impenetrable, even more unique, and it is this dark and menacing domain, entirely defined by this unknown age, that we are stepping into every time we mention his name. So in a way, it can be said that the actual history of Set has been traced throughout the ages through the constant effort the Egyptian people put throughout the entire history of their civilization to keep repairing his image and update his meaning according to how times were changing, without ever altering his essence as the unexpected, the one that could never become familiar or tamed. This is a direct parallel to what his unworldly existence was always there to mean, to remind us to keep our eyes constantly turned toward the shadows, opened to see what couldn't possibly be expected.

As we define ourselves as adepts of the Draconian Tradition, which is heavily toned by its dynamism and promises us constant challenges and changes of paradigm, and as magicians on the Left-Hand Path in general, walking against the very current of the cosmos, it should be easy then to think we are set on that way, that we can't possibly become stale, predictable, or addicted to a single way of thinking and seeing things. Unfortunately, nothing could be further from the truth as that very cosmic current we are set against is the one of creation and stability, constantly trying to define things, to solidify all, and a continuous opposition to all our efforts toward dissolution and freedom. To keep the shadow doors of mystery constantly opened is a constant struggle. It takes always looking into different directions, always rechecking and asking questions, again and again, knowing nothing is too established that it cannot crumble in a second of a direct attack. Keeping with this general principle, and knowing how it stems from the very nature of Set, it seems fitting to talk about him applying these two mechanisms, looking at what is often overlooked, trying to collect something that might be useful to create a strong contrast with the usual and put in check that which is the hardest of all to subject to: ourselves and the ideas we are used to accept and repeat.

Usually, when we are dealing with an Egyptian context, and we think of a guardian, the first name that naturally springs to our minds is probably that of Anubis, who fits that archetype so well. He is impassible, always watchful of his duty, and a constant reminder that traveling the ascending direction of the Nile, i.e. entering the Higher Waters, the magical domain usually hidden to our eyes, will be difficult and menacing. In the older, most primitive legends, though, the ascension toward higher planes was symbolized by a set of vertical stairs, which Horus would climb in order to keep up with his solar cosmic traveling. The guardian of those stairs was none other than Set himself, at this stage not displaying any enmity toward Horus, and being instead a helper and stage for the other god's journey. Even though these legends, given their status as even more impenetrable and mysterious than the other, most recent and well-known Egyptian legends concerning these gods, are not commonly mentioned and referenced in modern occult works. Their relationship to Set as he is mostly known in the Draconian Path, as the body, the essence of the path itself, and of the

Nightside, is quite striking. It seems more useful to focus our attention on this ancient, largely forgotten aspect of the god, which hits us quite close to home even if coming from that amazing distance.

The spiritual dimension and undertaking represented as the river, the Nile, in most Egyptian symbols, is full of important hints and relevant traces of spiritual science, but if we focus on the stairs for a second to attune ourselves to the arcane vibration of this older set of symbols, we may find some strong connections to the Kundalini work, since vertical ascendance in an initiatic context is always closely connected to the Axis Mundi. This absolutely rigid structure of reality, the sustaining pole, is described as the origin of all light and fire, holding the infinite cycles of transformation with its unyielding power. The cosmos may open in all directions, may expand eternally, but never breaks or becomes separated from its defining source. The path to this dimension, where time and space cease to exercise the plasticity that defines them and focus on absolute objectivity, is the Axis Mundi, where all subjectivity, doubts, confusion, contradictions, hesitations and comings and goings of the world become the inexorable, all-pervading, totality of will and spirit, impossible to divide and redirect anywhere but above. This is the perfect image of the magus, one with the spiritual realm installed in its life-giving existence.

This same nature, and the connection to the Axis Mundi, is found in us in the Susumna, the axis of our composite bodies, bringing our spiritual, soulful and physical natures to a whole. The fallen, powerless state of man happened when we turned away from its unity and chose to live by being moved around by the dangling, undefined currents of the Ida and Pingala, and the divine state, that which is aware of its power over the three domains that constitute us. It is regained when we turn back to the Susumna. The very word currently suggests a watery nature and explains to us how the Ida and

Pingala work. They are unsure, dependent on each other's behavior. The Pingala is responsible for our active side, our impulses to go forward and cause things around us, courage and determination, while the Ida is our receptive, passive side, constantly aware of the shortcomings and powerlessness that surrounds us - it is unfulfilled desire and absence. Those two are essentially linked, and the existence of one prevents the other from taking over and becoming an actual, outward power. They are the decisive step and the undying fear of not getting there, interlaced into one. All our ordinary thoughts, and the common, mundane constitution of humanity, are but the pendulum swing between a problem impossible to solve as long as we have our minds at it. The Kundalini awakening is a god-like process in which we suspend the loop which is entrapping our will, freezing, or stopping by an act of will and awareness of the watery flow of the Ida and Pingala. Beyond them, all we can see is the unshakeable Susumna, the unified principle that does not need contradiction in order to be.

The old Egyptians may not have been aware or connected to the Kundalini symbol as such, as no historical evidence shows that, but the Kundalini principle and the practices of Tantra Yoga are a crystallization of many other ancient practices and symbols. The basis for these practices was the mechanism of the male and female currents being in opposition that cannot be solved and will keep us enslaved to their indecision. This is attested all throughout sacred sciences over the world, undoubtedly constituting a part of what receives the name of Sophia Perennis: traces of sacred knowledge aspersed, always the same, even if presented differently throughout many different emanations and iterations around the world and over time. The caduceus of Hermes may be the most overt example of it, but it can also be seen in the alchemical symbolism of the pelican who bleeds one white drop and one red, the colors being classically associated with femininity and masculinity.

It becomes quite evident that the notion of Set, with all his restlessness and intensely virile essence, standing on the middle of the stairs, is what connects him to the sacred and is deeply related to the notion of the Axis Mundi or the Susumna in the Kundalini practices. It is also interesting to pick up on the contrast between the Ida and Pingala being watery in nature, and the Susumna dry - like the desert.

Now, another question that cannot but be asked whenever dealing with a guardian is what they are guarding, and, quite often more importantly, why they are guarding it. If Set is guarding the stairs between this world and the next, between the sacred and the profane, he also represents exactly what can shift us from one world to the next, and his essence and core are not only of the guardian but also of the gate itself, and even the very transition. Before the point he guards there is one, and right after the other one starts. As in the case of any guardian, there are things that will be allowed to pass, and those that will not. We, as humans, absolutely can pass since we are of a spiritual nature essentially, and we are only rightfully moving toward our natural home as we climb the stairs leading above. The role of the guardian is to show that the things that will not be allowed to pass can only be things present in ourselves but not in fact a part of us. The guardian, however, is not merely a function, because all of these are symbols and tools which must speak to us by their very nature, not things that simply perform a function, since the heart of the universe is that of meaning, not a Cartesian clock with things just fitting together in order to reach some obscure, unpronounced end. Then, if Set was chosen as the guardian, or was naturally put there by the universal order, the nature of Set and his attributes are an eloquent language telling us what to do, and in this case, what to leave behind so we can pass and become more than what we would be if we limited our existence to this plane alone.

Then we see Set as the Lord of Chaos, a pillar of determination and fierceness, able to defy the cosmic order and be the opposite of all other gods. He sets his self-proclaimed existence as an ever-changing cosmic stream whose only direct definition is that of having no definition. His eternal unfolding as a divine being asserts itself as far as the extension of mystery can go - that is, endlessly. The opposition and contradiction, of course, is here essential and well known to us all, but what is not often as much considered is what comes after the opposition, and how that opposition can be seen as another aspect of him as a guardian. We then realize that the antinomianism of Set, his nature of constant opposition and contradiction, may be both something we embody and oppose, contradicting things around us which are not useful anymore. These are the corpses we carry inside because something made us fall in love more with death than with life, and we seek the living among the dead so we can ascend. But, as we are also still living the process of abandonment and rebirth, the fatal stare of Set is also turned toward us, and he is opposing that which we are at this point, challenging it, threatening it, and quite possibly even attacking it when we invoke him and stand before him. There is a point in which we can become him, and be one with him, but until we do we can also be his prey, the one facing him as the guardian of the Other Side, and having to hear that we cannot pass unless we engage in a battle with him. Because we are at that present moment what cannot enter the sacred, we must become something else, which is what the Dragon does first and foremost. It is its defining feature which we call upon each time we enter our temples for a ritual.

We look deep into Set's eyes and see the before and the after. His strikes may hurt, confuse, or even lead us to question if we should be doing this in the first place. It is only divine love, though, as gods have no understanding of our lies and our illusions. They are as blind to our excuses as a person who doesn't know that water can satiate thirst. The fact that there is a set of stairs leading up reminds us that the divine nature is that of lightness, weightlessness of fire and of a sudden thunder, as no one would attempt to climb anything taking more baggage than what is truly needed. Going up is a process of exclusion first and foremost, and leaving the excessive weight behind is the first step on the journey. The menacing nature of a predator is what defines the god representing the entrance to that way. This reminds us to always fight for our survival, to act so with that same brutal immediacy we respond with when a living coal falls on our lap, and to never cease in our struggle for divinity and transcendence - the most important survival of all, that of our soul. First we have to react to the coal so that it doesn't burn our lap anymore. However, the divine fire burns forever and restlessly, so it will be ready to burn us for eternity unless we become that fierce beast that is focused on survival at every living minute. We must construct our mystical bodies - which are the instrument for the art - by doing the actual work as we stand in a temple - with limbs that are constantly ready to jump and attack in an instant, because our hunger cannot be satiated and there is no point in ever allowing ourselves to be still or morose about it. Then we can cross that threshold in which the ultimate Adversary will turn his attention to us, with divine eyes which can see all that we would rather keep hidden. In order for us to pass we must withstand the precision of that attack, which knows us better than we know ourselves, and the sculpting of our hearts by claws sharper than anything this world can know. We learn to be violent and restless by being submitted to the violence and restlessness of that passage, and if we survive and allow ourselves to be as dynamic and multiform as the Dragon, and look beyond the fake opposition that alienates us from the spirit, we can see we are both the hunter and the prey at the same time. This is what we need to survive on the journey ahead: the strength and the undying will, hunting ceaselessly what needs to die and rot in us, what makes us a helpless prey, what we will never pity to slaughter. We stand and go beyond, and when the Neters throw down their spears and water heavens with their tears, we will be what remains.

THE GODS
OF THE UNDERWORLD

Bill Duvendack

Nephthys

Originally a member of the Ennead from Heliopolis, she is first written about in the fifth dynasty pyramid texts, written approximately the 25th-mid-24th centuries BCE. Nephthys is, of course, her Greek name, as her original is Nebet-het, or Nebt-Het. Both translate to something similar to "lady of the house." Grossly misinterpreted in many neo-pagan circles as meaning the home and domestic life, this term actually means something deeper. In ancient Egypt the house could just as easily refer to a temple, so in that context she is a goddess of the temple, or in other words, a priestess. So let's just clarify here that if she is important enough to have withstood the test of time until now, it probably wasn't her ability in the kitchen that allowed that to happen! She is a priestess in her own right. What is she a priestess of, you may be wondering? Patience, because I will get to that in a moment, but there is something else that needs addressed first, in the name of context.

Factual evidence tells us that the oldest references to her date back to the 5th dynasty, or approximately 2499 BCE-2300 BCE. Yes, this is a broad range of dates, but it is accurate enough for our purposes. As we explored in the Sphinx Cell, the true, grasping roots of the solar-phallic paradigm were approximately the 4th dynasty, circa 27th BCE century-26th BCE century, so when we put the pieces together, we see that she has not been around as long as other Egyptian deities. This does not work against her, though, as her role fulfills an archetype that was around long before she arrived. While she only dates back to that time period, the true roots of her archetype go back into the mists of antiquities. As long as there has been a dark goddess female priestess on the planet, she has been there, lurking in the shadows, developing in potency. However, this particular time period is interesting because this was a transitional period, so in some ways she could be seen as a harbinger of things to come, or a transitional being in the same way as Hermanubis. Thus, she can be seen as a priestess ushering in the age of Osiris. We must also remember that changes like these didn't happen overnight nor during one dynasty, but rather over an extended period of time. She was one of the markers of the rise of the cult of Osiris.

There is something important to note here, though, and that is that while that is true, it is also true that there were female priestesses long before her. In a lot of ways, what we see with her is the creation of an archetype. It is with her that we see that she is the individuation of the archetype of the female priestess figure. What makes her unique, though, is that she is a dark goddess priestess, specifically of death. Her role usually had to do with the funerary process, as she worked hand in hand with Anpu quite a bit in various texts and mortuary depictions. As a matter of fact, her relationship with Anpu is a lot closer than that, as she was his mother in some stories.

Also, in accord with some stories, she is known as the wife of her brother Set. These stories come from Heliopolis, and in other places, there were other stories. In one reference, the wife of Set was a goddess named Horea, but not much has survived past just her name and place. Nephthys is generally known as the wife and sister of Set, the two of them being of the four children of Geb and Nuit, according to the stories. While this wasn't the only lineage of hers, it is the most popular one today. In the oldest stories, Nephthys was not the consort of Set. This was an addition that came much later, and this is worth noting because his original wife was most likely Horea, who history has swallowed. Thus, we can see that as the Age of Osiris came into being, she was elevated and changed. Another radical but interesting point to consider is that often times the name "Nephthys" is seen as a title because of its original meaning and translation. This would be similar to how the name Lucifer is a title. The radical notion that goes along with this is that there may be a goddess named "Horea, Nebet-Het," which would translate to "Horea, the Lady of the House." This is interesting to ponder because it would show the two are blended together, and that both would be indicative of a wife of Set. Does this actually exist in ancient Egypt? To my knowledge no, but it is something to think about none the less. This would also give Horea more weight and credence than just the wife of Set. It would establish her as a priestess in her own right, which is more fitting of being the wife of Set. If we think about that, we can deduce that she would be a priestess of one of the characteristics of Set, so she may be a priestess of storms, or of the desert, or of one of the many other functions Set has served throughout the centuries.

At this point you may be asking yourself why I have put so much effort into discussing Nephthys in an anthology about Set, so let us turn our attention to this. Originally Set was the god of the desert and of storms. His characteristics of chaos and the equivalent of the Christian devil came later with the pollution of monotheism and eventually the Greeks. However, energetically speaking, these two are connected in a lot of ways and thus can be worked with in tandem. Regardless of which face of his you look at, his benevolent role as a protector of the solar barque or his role as a god of storms and the desert, you see parallels between the two of them.

Nephthys is a dark goddess and Set is a dark god. True, in his earliest role he would have been more neutral, because the desert and storms have a similar meaning as symbols. It is the reaction of humans to these events that dictate whether they are malevolent or benevolent. The dark nature of Nephthys' character had to do with the funerary and embalming processes that occurred at the end of life. She is known as the twin sister of Aset, AKA Isis, so as much as Aset represents life, Nephthys represents death. This is worth pointing out because, in fact, death is neutral as well, as it accepts all and is simply a part of life. Both are initiatic deities, Set in the way that he initiated Ra's solar barque through the Duat, and Nephthys due to her role as death priestess, initiating the body into the afterlife. Both of them have to do with the underworld and the Duat as well, generally performing psychopomp roles routinely. If you choose to see that she is not the wife of Set, then you should feel free to do so. However, if you prefer to work with both of them together, then feel free! There is no dogma in this case because of the various pantheons and length of the Egyptian empire, so a lot of this is personal preference. You should also decide whether or not you see her as the mother of Anpu, too, because this addresses another facet of Set's character, the role of fatherhood.

Now that those questions are settled, let's discuss the two of them together. She is the female necromancer in a lot of ways, a priestess of death. We know that Set is an expert warrior, which means he is highly familiar with death in his own way. Therefore, another shared characteristic they have is that of death. Brutal, thorough, death. They are both twins of the Heliopolitan counterparts, Aset and Asar, Isis and Osiris, respectively. This is important to the proactive researcher because it tells us if we want to know more about Set and Nephthys, we can also look at Asar and Aset. Asar is a god of life, Set is a god of death. The same is true for Aset and Nephthys in that they are polar opposites in that regard. It is theorized that she was created as the female counterpart to Set in as many ways as possible. Set was barren, she was barren. You can see how this contradicts the story of her being the mother of Anpu. Set was the desert, she the air. However, in other places she corresponds to water due to her nature focused around death and dying. Her animal association is the vulture. Whether you work with them as a married couple or not, you can still work with them together by addressing one of their shared correspondences as a focal point.

Another part of her character that fits in well with Set is that she is the patron goddess of the Bennu bird. The Bennu bird was the ancient Egyptian word for a sacred phoenix. This tells us she corresponds to the life, death, rebirth process of change. Being a harbinger and instigator of change is a title for Set as well, so by working with the two, you can increase your ability to navigate periods of change. You also increase your ability to come out ahead when it is all said and done.

Of course, there I am discussing the great transformation known as death in a symbolic context, but there is also the very literal way, too. Both of them could be worked with regarding death and dying. Remember, though, that capacity is somewhat limited due to the role of Anpu and Asar. Set would be the bringer of death, and Nephthys would be the mistress of the funerary process and last rites. As a matter of fact, those that did her work, so to speak, in ancient Egypt, were known as the "Hawks of Nephthys." Interestingly enough, she is also the goddess of rain, and Set the god of storms.

This also means she is a patroness of necromancers, too, which is quite fascinating because so many patrons of necromancers are generally men. Yes, Anpu would be seen as a patron god of necromancers, but in the case of ancient Egypt you have a patron for each sex as seen above. This puts Set in the role of being associated with death but not necessarily necromancy.

Another minor part of her character that oftentimes gets glossed over is her prowess as a warrior. In the oldest texts, she was depicted as fighting alongside with Set to protect Ra's barque as it travels through the Duat, defending it from Apophis. This tells us she can be used as a goddess of war and violence if desired. This is a common trait she shares with Set - violence. Another trait she shares with him for our purposes is that of darkness and night.

Finally, we come to an interesting connection she has, which is to Atlantis. According to Lewis Spence, there was a temple to Nephthys on the North African coast to the west of Alexandria. There stood a pillar that had hieroglyphs that discussed Atlantis and the relationship Egypt had to it. However, the temple and entire city was lost to an earthquake that buried it, and it remains hidden to this day. This tells us she can be worked with in order to gain access to very ancient information.

The Dark Halves

The information about Nephthys discussed above is necessary to not only come to know her more thoroughly, but also to reveal her true face. For the rest of this essay we are going to look at the relationship between her and Set, which means we will be operating from the perspective that she is his wife, which means working with the Heliopolis Ennead. I choose this because this is the story most people are familiar with, even if they don't know the particulars. Approaching their story from this perspective also states we will be working with the concept that Aset and Asar, Nebet-het and Set, all balance each other out through being counterparts. A deeper metaphysical truth is being conveyed here, but we won't necessarily go into that depth. Simply know there are deeper levels for the intrepid explorer.

Let's start off by discussing fertility. Both Nephthys and Set were known as barren, and Set was potentially even gay or bisexual. That characteristic is not discussed to my knowledge about Nephthys, but logic says she would be the same. But if she was barren, then how was she the mother of Anpu? The story, according to legend, is that she impersonated Aset/Isis and seduced Asar/Osiris. This was easy for her to do because she is her twin. Some variations say she drugged him, while others leave it unclear. Regardless, Anpu was born out of that union as the story goes, but there is no explanation how he was conceived if she was barren. You can see how different variations of the surviving stories occasionally come into conflict with each other. Another part of the story is that this affair was the motivation for the killing of Asar by Set, but this is not discussed in other legends.

Also remember that it was the two of them that were defending Ra's barque, so in this way they could be seen as a warrior couple. So to recap, they are the dark god and dark goddess couple of ancient Egypt. They are warriors. They both correspond to features of storms, in that Set is the god of storms, and Nebet-het is the goddess of rain and air. Both are deities of death as well, but the difference is that she is more necromantic whereas he is not. They both work with the rites of death, though, just in different capacities, for his arts are more martial than hers, but hers are more magical. Together they give us insight into a very interesting perspective from ancient Egypt, not only on the darker nature of things, but also on their understanding of how people complement each other.

They are the dark to the light of Aset and Asar. Symbolically, though, they are representative of the transfer of power from Draconian times to the solar phallic paradigm that came in with the rise of the age of Osiris, so in this way she and Set give us insight into what was around before. There is one striking difference between her and Set, though, and that is that she is a protectress of life as much as death. There are many recorded instances of her role of watching over newborns hand in hand with Aset. Regardless of his correspondences, Set is generally not seen as a protector of newborns. He is seen as the defender of the light, though.

THE DARK GOD AND GODDESS OF ANCIENT EGYPT

A Ritual

In a broad sense we could say that these two are the dark god and goddess of ancient Egypt, especially if you give credence to the Heliopolis story. This could be particularly useful for modern neopagans, especially the ones that enjoy working with the Egyptian pantheon, because it gives counterparts to a degree that has not really been discussed before. It helps to form a cohesive pantheon. Is it traditional Egyptian? Nope, not at all. However, isn't it conceptually more in line with the ancient Egyptian idea of the Duat? Without question. Regardless of whether or not you experiment with this, it is smart to note this because it tells us there are layers and mysteries of ancient Egyptian spirituality that we cannot fathom, but through exploration we come a little closer to understanding, even if it is through non-traditional means. There are many spiritual secrets that are still concealed that date back to that time period, and it is only through exploration that we uncover them for ourselves. In the following ritual, you will make contact with the two of them in their dark goddess and god roles in the ancient Egyptian underworld. This ritual is to be performed at a new moon. The only light for the ritual is what is necessary for reading the ritual. For incense, use either dragon's blood or frankincense and myrrh. The candles are to be black, or if you can produce it, with black flames. Have the sigil of the temple on the altar, and feel free to add visual depictions of these two as well. If you have any other symbols that have to do with Set and Nephthys, feel free to add them.

Begin the ritual by cleansing your ritual space with the incense. Face west, and travel clockwise with the incense, honoring the quarters as you go. Call your guardians as you choose, but it would be wise to make them Egyptian whenever possible. When you return to the west, place your incense in its proper place on the altar. Turn your attention to the images that represent them on your altar. As you do, invoke them, one at a time, into you and invite them into your temple. When you feel their presence, continue.

Trace a sickle in the air above the altar. Use either your wand, incense stick, or actual sickle. While tracing it, chant "Tua Nebet-het, tua Set!" This translates to "Adorations to Nephthys! Adorations to Set!" When this is done, chant "Oes-tu, sexem!" This translates to: "Rise up, conquer!" While you chant this, visualize achieving your goal and manifesting your results. Continue chanting this as you gaze at the images of the two. Continue to chant until you feel your message has been transmitted and received in the Duat. When you feel the energy is charged in your temple and they are close, state your intent. When you have done this, execute the confession.

This is something that was common in ancient Egyptian rituals, and it served as a form of confession/purification. During that time it may have been known as a personal exorcism, in that the individual is exorcising their own demons. Here is an example: "I stand before you, pure of heart and mind, in the presence of the gods! I stand here cleansed before you, voicing my will." Feel free to use this or to create your own, but the point of it is to purify thyself in the presence of the gods.

When this is done, trace an ankh in the air above the altar. Then say "By my will it is done!" Close your ritual space in the fashion you prefer. Remember to give thanks and praises to the deities invoked at the quarters. Follow this with a cleansing of the space using incense as was done at the beginning of the ritual. Record the results in your journal and return to your everyday life. This ritual serves as contact with those two deities, and to invite them into your space to work with you over the next four weeks at most, two weeks minimum.

SET AND NEPHTHYS CHAOS AND VOID

Asenath Mason

While there is a lot of information about Set, the Egyptian Lord of Darkness, and we can also find some sources on Nephthys, his sister-consort, the connection between them is rarely explored, especially from a magical perspective. In this article I would like to give this subject a little more attention, presenting ideas on how this connection can be used in a practical way. What you will find here is based on my personal work with both god-forms, and I encourage the reader to explore and develop the concept presented here through your own practice.

Set is a god of many faces and even more aspects and magical powers. For the purpose of this ritual, however, we will focus on his role of the god of storm and chaos. This aspect is strong from the first moment he comes into being. Instead of being born in the normal manner, like his siblings, he tears himself out of his mother's womb. But before we proceed to discussing his violent nature, let us say a few words about his mythology and background. As you may already know,

Set was one of the children of the sky goddess Nut and the earth god Geb, born together with Isis, Osiris, and Nephthys, who became his wife and life companion. Therefore, originally, he was one of the earliest gods of ancient Egypt. His name was alternatively spelled Seth, Setekh, Sut, Sutekh, and Suty, and he was believed to preside over storms, wind, chaos, and violence. This was not necessarily viewed in a negative way, and Set was often seen as a strong and powerful god, protector of pharaohs and a heroic chief deity. At the time of the Hyksos dynasty he was the chief god of the pantheon and his cult flourished across the land. That time, however, was also when his role was demonized, and after the conquest of Egypt by foreign nations such as the Assyrian empire, he became associated with foreign oppressors and recognized as the god of the foreigners and the lord of the hostile desert.

He rules over eclipses, thunderstorms and earthquakes, and in the Book of the Dead he is called "the Lord of the Northern Sky." As a god of destruction, he is associated with fire and red color - the red desert, the bloodshed in a battle, the scorching sun of the midday, etc. - and in depictions he is often portrayed with red hair signifying his violent, fiery nature. This aspect of Set appears throughout a number of myths and legends. One of the most known stories is his murder and mutilation of his brother Osiris. No less important is the myth of rivalry between him and Horus in the struggle for the throne of Osiris. The Egyptians even believed that the two would continue their conflict until the end of time, when chaos swallowed the order of Ma'at and primordial waters would flood the whole world. In various versions of the myth, Horus either defeats Set, representing good triumphing over evil, or their battle never ends, signifying the eternal struggle between chaos and order or darkness and light. In many of these myths, however, Set's role is not negative, and he is presented as the lord of the red (desert) land and the balance to Horus as the lord of the black (soil) land. In the same positive sense he is sometimes presented as a friend of the dead, helping them ascend to heaven on his ladder, the crowner of pharaohs, and the leader of warriors.

In the Book of the Dead, Set himself claims to be "the originator of confusion who thunders in the horizon of heaven," and this aspect is strongly emphasized in his mythology. Even the hieroglyph that symbolized the god was often used in words such as "confusion," "turmoil," and "rage," and sometimes also "sickness." He was believed to be responsible for the hot desert wind, drought, and the burning sun that dried the land and brought death to vegetation and famine to people and animals. He was the lowering clouds at the horizon, his voice was the sound of thunder, and his wrath was believed to cause the earth to tremble. In this sense, he resembles Typhon of Greek mythology, and when his role was demonized, these two mythological figures were believed to be one and the same. We might even say that Set's appearance, which has never been identified with any existing animal, points at his primordial character. Dragons, serpents, monsters, and various hybrids appearing in world's mythologies usually represent the original chaos - that which is unfamiliar, unknown, illogical, irrational, and impossible to describe or grasp in full. Set's face, which bears certain similarities to some animals and yet cannot be fully identified with any, seems to reflect the same idea. As a personification of chaos, he exists outside the order of Ma'at, without being subjected to any laws or limitations, which is reflected in both his actions and appearance. He can do things others cannot and as a self-created god he is a powerful archetype of the Adversary. On the other hand, Set himself fights with chaos, protecting the sun god Ra in the underworld while traveling with him each night in the Barque of Millions of Years. Each time Ra descends to the underworld he is attacked by Apep, and each time his companions help him in this fight, but only Set is powerful enough to slay the serpent of chaos.

In rites of magic, Set as a lord of chaos often comes like a tornado, destroying a lot of things in the practitioner's life and making way for others to manifest. His energy is fiery, fierce and furious. It shakes the world around us like an earthquake, destroys foundations and life-stability, connections and relationships, but at the same time opens many new doors and creates new opportunities. This energy is also masculine and often aggressive, provoking fights and confrontations in our daily situations, or prompting us to seek our personal power through harsh life ordeals. Set represents change, movement and transition. He is an enemy of stagnation, destroyer of predictability and bringer of chaos. This aspect of the god is often viewed as confusing and dangerous because what we usually want is stability and safety. He destroys all that, shaking the very foundations of our universe and prompting us to move forward. This sudden arrival of chaos and confusion is sometimes needed in our life, and we can invoke Set whenever we need a change in our environment, but the way it happens is not always easy for us to deal with it. Here is where the gnosis of Nephthys comes useful - she represents the center of chaos, the point of stillness among confusion, the eye of the tornado.

The role of this dark goddess is often underestimated, and she is either overshadowed by her sister Isis or mentioned merely as the consort of Set and pushed into the background. Sometimes she is paired with Isis as her dark twin and portrayed as darkness complementary to the light of the goddess of life and magic. This is an important function, but her connection with Set is just as essential to the understanding of her role in the initiatory magic of the Left Hand Path.

What we know about Nephthys from myths and historical accounts shows her as a goddess of death, lamentation and funerary rites. She is a "friend of the dead" and a companion of the deceased, offering guidance to the newly dead and comfort to the relatives of the one who died. As the sister of Isis, she stands for magic and the power of transformation, and she can endow the practitioner with the ability to see that which is "hidden by moonlight" - awakening the psychic senses and opening the mind for the vision of the astral world. As the mother of Anubis, the lord of the dead, she is associated with necromancy and death mysteries. Her hair is compared to the strips of cloth that shroud the mummy, she protects the earthly vessel of the deceased soul, and along with Hapi she guards the lungs in their canopic jar on the north cardinal point. As the goddess of death and funerary rites, she assists Isis in gathering the dismembered parts of the body of Osiris after he is murdered by Set and preparing them for the proper burial.

In rites of magic, Nephthys appears as the Lady of the Temple, the Goddess of Darkness and the Mistress of Sacrifice. She arises from the night as a woman with black feathered wings, cloaked in darkness or surrounded by a thick black mist. Her astral energy is black, and she often comes with spectral shades that assume the form of snakes or winged creatures. These nocturnal entities are extensions of her nighttime current, often manifesting in rites of evocation to speak on behalf of the goddess. They also reflect her primordial nature, showing that she is one of the primal Ophidian/Draconian deities. Sometimes she appears with a chalice, which is symbolic of her feminine nature, but unlike the chalices of other dark goddesses, often filled with either poison or nectar, her vessel is empty and represents the void. The goddess herself resides in the center of nothingness, surrounded by the chaos of Set, or we might say that she is the void while Set is chaos and confusion. When we invoke Set and let his chaos enter our life, many things are brought to the surface - thoughts, emotions, perceptions, beliefs, etc. - but they all eventually become absorbed by the vacuum of Nephthys. This is a purifying experience, like death and rebirth in a mystical sense. Seen from this perspective, the goddess stands for a devouring principle, gaping womb that gives birth to chaos and releases it into the world through Set, but then she absorbs it back to the source to cleanse and refine all that is brought with it. While Set is chaos, she is stillness. When Set is the storm, she is calmness. Set represents manifestation, and she is nothingness, the void, the zero point. She is all and nothing at the same time - the vacuum, the eye in the center of the tornado.

The sigil used in this ritual reflects the concept of the goddess as the central point of chaos as well. It includes the eye of the goddess, which stands for self-awareness and awakened consciousness, surrounded by four pyramids pointing in the four cardinal directions to show that we are dealing here with the concept of the center. The circle around it represents continuity and the eternal cycle of the universe, while the snakes, depicted in anticlockwise movement, typify the chaotic forces of Set and point at the Ophidian/Draconian character of his current.

You can perform the following working when you seek understanding of chaos and confusion that is already happening in your life or to balance the energy released by invoking Set through any of the rituals presented in this book. You can also use it to invoke the chaos of Set into your life through the balancing force of Nephthys. This will become useful if you seek ideas or inspiration in your life or new directions in your magical work. You can then invoke Set for the purpose of brainstorming and Nephthys to find clarity and understanding in chaos and confusion. Feel free to experiment with both approaches and explore the connection between Set and Nephthys through your personal work. You will find rituals invoking Set earlier in this book, while this working is centered on Nephthys as a complementary force to the current of the god of chaos.

Preparations

Prepare yourself for this working by meditating on the sigil provided here and chanting the mantra "Pert em kerh, Sutuach! Pert em kerh, Nebet-Het!" This should be done at least on the day preceding the actual ritual, but you can also dedicate more days to this working and meditate on the sigil for as long as it takes to attune yourself to the currents of both god-forms. For these meditations you will only need one black candle, representing the darkness of the goddess, and the sigil, which should be painted in gold on a black background. If you work with incense, the best choice is Dragon's Blood or a blend called the Nile Temple, but you can also use frankincense or myrrh.

Take the sigil into your hand, or place it in front of you, and gaze at it until you can memorize its shape. At the same time, chant the mantra and focus on the energies of Set and Nephthys flowing through the sigil into your temple and back - taking your intent to the Other Side. You can also anoint the sigil with a few drops of your blood if you want to. Then blow out the candle and meditate in darkness. See the sigil burning in front of you, moving and morphing into a vortex of chaos. This is the current of Set. In the center of this vortex you can see Nephthys - stillness in the middle of confusion. Open yourself to her consciousness and focus on how it feels to be inside the storm, the eye of the tornado. Feel the calmness and tranquility that comes with her energy, sense the soft breeze of her nighttime current on your skin, hear her voice speaking to you through your inner mind. Open yourself to her presence and embrace it. When you feel this presence leaving, close the working for the day.

Sigil of Nephthys and Set

The Ritual

When you feel ready to perform the ritual, begin the ceremony in the same way - prepare the sigil, light the black candle and burn the incense. For this working you will also need a chalice - fill it with wine or water and place it on the altar. A black chalice is the best choice for this ritual. Take a moment to attune yourself to the current of Nephthys and Set by gazing at the sigil and chanting their names. Then speak the following invocation:

> *I invoke Nephthys, Lady of Darkness,*
> *Mistress of the chalice and the tomb,*

Daughter of Nut and Geb, child of the earth and the sky!
Sister of Isis, wife of Set and mother of Anubis!
I summon the Black Mother,
Nephthys! Nebet-Het! Nebt-Het!
For I am ...(your magical name)...!

As you speak the words of invocation, visualize yourself inside a pyramid. It is dark and dusty and looks like a tomb. The sigil that you have been using in the workings is engraved on the floor. Stand in the center of it and visualize the goddess manifesting in front of you - a woman in a long black dress, with black hair and black eyes. She is surrounded by darkness which seems alive - it is moving and morphing into shapes of ghastly figures and faces. When you build this image in your mind and feel her presence in the ritual space, continue the invocation:

Lady of the Temple,
Hear my words and come to me!
Guide me through storm and confusion to clarity and
knowledge,
Lead me through darkness to light and through strife to
balance,
And help me find stillness in chaos and peace in turmoil,
For I stand before you ready to enter your inner sanctum,
To find wisdom and understanding in the heart of your
hallowed place.

Envision that the goddess opens her mouth and breathes out black spectral snakes made of shadow and smoke, forming a swirling vortex around you. They coil around you, press upon your skin, and finally merge with your aura. It feels like being filled with darkness. From this darkness inside you arises everything that is chaotic, confusing, unclear, threatening, etc. - images and thoughts of dark and chaotic things happening in your life, dark emotions, fears, and all that prevents you from moving forward. This experience can be intense and painful - let it happen. You can also choose to focus on one thing only, something that is bothering you at the moment, or a question to which you cannot find a clear answer. When you feel ready, continue the working:

Goddess of the Dark Side,
Transform and purify me through your rites of chaos and void,
Give me your eyes so I may pierce the veil of obscurity and find the answers I seek,
Protect and guide me on the Path of the Night,
And let me be reborn through the darkness of your black womb,
Where nothing exists and all comes to being.
In Nomine Draconis,
Ho Drakon Ho Megas!

Then visualize that the goddess opens her mouth again, but this time she breathes all the shadows in, absorbing and transforming them. Feel the darkness leaving you, taking away all thoughts, emotions and feelings. She sucks everything in, leaving you perfectly empty, like a vessel or shell, which feels calming and cleansing. This is a state of perfect tranquility and clarity. You can now look at your questions and issues as if they were not part of you but outside of you, while you yourself remain in the center - in perfect control of your life. Perhaps this will give a fresh perspective and help you find the answers and solutions you seek. Blow out the candle and meditate in darkness to fully attune yourself to the energies of the goddess. You can also take some personal time with her for meditation or conversation and open yourself for any messages she may have for you. When you feel ready to finish the working, thank the goddess for her presence with a few personal words, and close the ritual by saying:

And so it is done.

CONTRIBUTORS
TEMPLE OF ASCENDING FLAME

Asenath Mason is a writer and artist. Author of books and essays on esoteric, religious and mythological subjects, with a particular focus on the Left Hand Path philosophy, Luciferian Spirituality and Draconian Tradition. Active practitioner of Occult Arts. Founder and coordinator of the Temple of Ascending Flame. Author of *The Book of Mephisto: A Modern Grimoire of the Faustian Tradition* (2006), *Necronomicon Gnosis: A Practical Introduction* (2007), *Sol Tenebrarum: The Occult Study of Melancholy* (2011), *The Grimoire of Tiamat* (2013), *Liber Thagirion* (2014), *Draconian Ritual Book* (2016), *Qliphothic Meditations* (2016), *Qliphothic Invocations & Evocations* (2017), *Rituals of Pleasure* (2018), co-author of *Chants of Belial* (2016, in collaboration with Edgar Kerval), *Dream Gates & Astral Paths* (2019, also with Edgar Kerval), and *Awakening Lucifer* (2017, with Bill Duvendack), and co-author and editor of a number of anthologies and occult magazines. Co-owner of Draco Press. She is also a varied artist, working with digital media, and themes of her artwork include various gothic, fantasy and esoteric concepts.
Contact: **facebook.com/asenathmason.official**
Art: **asenathmason.darkfolio.com**
Books, art, consultations: **becomealivinggod.com/asenathmason**

Bill Duvendack is an astrologer, internationally known psychic, presenter, teacher, and author. He is also a Thelemic bishop. He has presented in many venues, ranging from colleges and high schools to national and international conferences. He is the author of the published books "Vocal Magick," "The Metaphysics of Magick," "In the Shadow of the Watchtower, Enochian Grimoire Volume 1," "Dark Fruit, Enochian Grimoire Volume 2," "Spirit Relations," "Awakening Lucifer," "Sat En Anpu" a book on Anubis, and "Astrology in Theory and Practice." He has had over two dozen essays published in various anthologies, and his magical writings have been translated into 6 languages. He regularly teaches classes on magick, astrology, and modern spirituality, nationally and digitally. He is also the co-owner of Draco Press and high priest of the Temple of Ascending Flame. He has been interviewed by the NY Times, RTE 1, and has made many TV and radio appearances. For more information about him, please consult his website: **www.418ascendant.com**

Cătălina Deaconu was attracted quite young by the entropic gravitation of the Black Sun and delved right into the Draconic mysteries just as she began her Initiatic journey, captured all the way from the extremely suggestive and mysterious land of Romania, where she was born and still lives. Taking a quick look away from the drudgeries of ordinary life, her avid, sharp eyes and her inexorable desire for excellence and absolute transcendence drove her attention to the Left Hand Path almost immediately, after just a few months of studying Magic in general. The Dragon's promise of power and victory turned her so intensely that she is entirely dedicated to the practices of the Temple of the Ascending Flame, guided by the Luciferian wisdom of Asenath Mason, Kenneth Grant and Michael Kelly. The qliphothic venom has found its way deeply into her life, causing indescribable changes and violating the lines between possible and impossible as she finishes her official studies, as well as her passionate discoveries within foreign languages, with the intent of taking the antinomian spirit with her into her chosen profession of a lawyer, as well as keeping it in all her future endeavors in the realms of art and literature. Website: **insidiousarrow.tumblr.com**

Edgar Kerval, from Colombia, South America. Musician, writer and artist focused on deconstructing different magickal vortices through deep states of consciousness and gnosis, reflected in his ritual project EMME YA, in which he focuses atavistic and chthonic energies to create vast soundscapes and ritual vaporous atmospheres. His other projects are THE RED PATH, THE RED ANGLE, NOX 210, :ARCHAIC:, SONS OV SIRIUS, LUX ASTRALIS, TOTEM..., to name a few. Edgar Kerval published his book *Via Siniestra - Under the Mask of the Red Gods* through Aeon Sophia Press, where he recorded his experiences with Qliphothic magick and energies from African and Brazilian sorcery that he called "The Red Gods." His second book called *Ast Ma Ion-Eos Tar Nixet* was released by Ophiolatreia Press. He also works on publications

such as *Qliphoth Journal*, *Noxaz* and *Sabbatica*. At the moment he is running his own publishing house, Sirius Limited Esoterica.
kerval111@gmail.com
facebook.com/edgar.kerval

Fra Diavolo is a German magician and occultist, working for almost 20 years in different areas of magic arts, covering Draconian and Luciferian Magic as well as Chaos Magic, Hermetics, Satanism, Setianism, Kabbalah and Qliphoth. He was initiated into different magic groups, such as the Temple of Ascending Flame. As an active member of these occult organizations he is working much with ritual magic, but beside this, he is also focusing on developing his own personal magical work.
Contact: **kuwen12@gmail.com**

Keona Kai'Nathera is a Satanic Daemonaltress and a HPS of the Brotherhood of Satan, a member of the Temple of Ascending Flame, member of the House of Delepitore and co-founder of The House of Baal. She practices Blood Magick, Divination, Vamprisim, Herbalism and Necromancy; and is a lifelong student in the Dark Arts.
Contact: **YouTube @Keona Esh IG @keonakainathera**
Website: **www.queensenigma.wordpress.com**

Mimi Hazim has held strong interest in occultic and spiritual practices since she was a child - it has been the one constant in her life. The areas of her experience include soul travel, multi-dimensional lives and realities, alchemy of the spirit, spiritual healing, as well as visionary technique and consciousness expansion. Through her experience, she has found the spiritual and magickal path to be one of true riches, accessible to those who hold the focus and desire to develop themselves on ever deeper levels of the waters of the psyche.
Mimi can be contacted at **MimiMay12@yahoo.co.uk**

Soror Sortela is a Canadian transgender occultist, writer and musician specializing in the Left-Hand Path tradition. She is the author of both "Liber Antichristos" and "True Black Magick: The Secret Art of the Ancient Adepts," expounding a unique manifestation of the Typhonian Tradition through a rigorous self-initiation curriculum of sexual alchemy. She is currently planning a reformation of this curriculum through her latest endeavor: Order of The Others, the goal of which is to establish proper cultural and magickal climates for traffic with Outside Forces.

Inquiries regarding previous publications or the Order of The Others may be sent to **jordano.bortolotto@gmail.com** with subject either being "Published Works" or "Order Inquiry."

V. Ghallego-Iglesias has been burning the Promethean fire and dedicating his life to the occult sciences since 2007, after being attracted to the Great Work by several tormenting months of obsessive apocalyptic dreams. Most of his work during this period has been along the side of Traditional Hermetic Orders, digging into the arcane roots that sustain the tree of Western Esotericism to this day. During this journey, the fruit of all delight was offered to him by the Dark Goddess manifesting as Lilith to him very soon, changing everything with her deadly and venomous beauty, which guided a great deal of his decisions and experiences ever since. This epiphany made him search throughout many years for a way to bring that essence into practical work, until the perfect marriage for his inspiration came in the way of the Temple of Ascending Flame, with which he has been working for a few months now, but already enough to feel like he's found a home. His magician's passion for spelling and riddles extends to all the domains of his life, with his day job of a translator and transcriptionist, and his developing works as an artist, in both literature and visual arts.

Website: **insidiousarrow.tumblr.com**

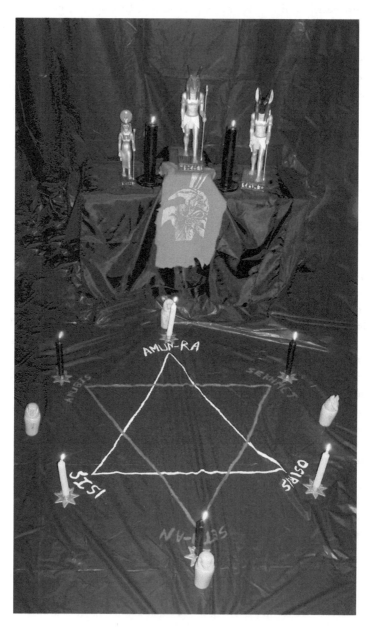

Sethanic Altar - Basic Circle

EGYPTIAN LEFT-HAND PATH MAGICK

THE NETER SET AND THE BLACK ALCHEMY OF THE BA AND KA

Michael W. Ford, Akhtya Dahak Azal'ucel,
Sasutekhwoser V°,
Priest of Heka, Priest of Set

Part 1. Luciferian and Sethanic Theory

Initiation is a self-determined act in the Left-Hand Path to begin a new path and journey toward actualization, toward ones' perceived potential, devoid of restrictive religious dogma. Luciferianism, like other LHP traditions, embraces the concept of spiritual dissent and self-liberation from restrictive beliefs, possible character flaws (when identified) or weaknesses to strive toward overcoming and enhancement of the individual by some level of Magick.

The 11 Points of Power, the foundation and simplification of Luciferian Philosophy, identify a structure of thinking and the way one perceives not only the self but also the world they live in (your daily life and those surrounding it) as crucial toward the Triad of the Morning Star. The Triad is a name for the simplified basic three spheres of practicing Luciferian Magick. These are recognizable and measurable levels which identify attainment and insight bringing awareness of existing as an isolate being. As an individual, you have the responsibility to strive toward adapting the 11 Points as a guideline only if you identify with most of the points. Some people are just not "wired" to be truly Left-Hand Path.

The spiritual linage of the modern Luciferian Tradition is found from the unique and individual adaptation as an expression of the Adversarial Current. While there are defined outlined ceremonies, rituals and traditions within our cultus, dogmatic stagnation is rejected by the self-determined adaptation of rites and workings done so to harmonize with the aspirations and predilection of the Luciferian.

The Black Adept perpetuates the focus of energy and its projection toward specific goals carefully identified and thus dedicated to attaining. This is the cycle of power by mental determination and discipline, which in response transmutes to reaching the first plateau of symbolically breaking a chain. This is a general experience of not only the identification but also having the determination and courage by consistent disciplined habit-breaking to attain Liberation. This is accomplished by small steps which increase the energy of you as a magician and are conjuring, shaping and directing it toward your chosen desire. To identify as a Luciferian, you must find a familiar structure of thinking and feel at ease with the 11 Points of Power.

Metaphorically, the spark of the Black Flame, the gift of Azazel and the Watchers of the tradition of Enoch, is in the nature of the sons or daughters of Cain, the first Satanist and Murderer, having the paternal lineage of a Spirit of Fire and Air, Samael, and descendants such as Tubal-Cain and Naamah (a Lilith-like demonic spirit). This Black Flame is a small essence of being awake, aware and inspired by the tools and traditions of Magick and Sorcery. This luminous fire is that which sets you apart (and often alone) from the crowd: a mentally strong individual who is not influenced by the popular opinions of the masses or what the media tells you is appropriate.

The Luciferian watches and discovers the basic tools of Luciferian Magick which are found as a result of applying the 11 Points of Power consistently. The method of perceiving not only your opinions, beliefs and outward ways in which you view the world is the most important method of initiation. There is a Word of Power which I discuss in some early workings and publications: AZOTHOZ. Azothoz is a word-sigil and formula which indicates that all BEGINS and ENDS with you. No deity, demon, spirit, or living person has the responsibility or even ability to cause good or bad things to happen from a "higher power" perspective. No deity can make something happen for you. This relies entirely upon the quality and skills of yourself as a Luciferian. Within the

Circle of Convocation, it is the Black Adept that directs the energies that are invoked. By fumigation (the offering of incense) and libation, this Black Alchemical process of internal and external change is honored.

You may in ritual invoke and offer libation or incense to a Deific Mask (Deity), accepting it as perhaps an archetype, a conscious spiritual being, or even a representation of a type of energy and power you encircle and direct toward a goal. When attained, you may desire to burn incense or pour a libation to the Deific Mask after achieving your desire, unless, of course, by way of intuition, you deem this unimportant. Azothoz is a cipher for the force or power within both nature and within us as the Adversary, more specifically, the Egyptian Neter (God) Set (or Seth, Set-Typhon or Sutekh among other names).

The Luciferian Tradition as reflected and presented in my publications has many paths and ancient traditions which contribute to our modern Left-Hand Path body of knowledge. One significant modern teaching and first acknowledged "Luciferian" structure of initiation was defined by the Sethanic Cult of Masks, directed and taught originally by Charles Pace, Hamar'at. He identified himself openly as a Priest of Seth and a Satanist in 1963.[1] Charles Pace was an expert on ancient Egyptian Magic (rejecting the Qabalah entirely) and contributed to early Wiccan covens founded by Gerald Gardner during that time.

The Sethanic Cult of Masks united rational, self-accountable, pragmatic thinking with the beauty and discipline of ceremonial magick and drawing the overlooked connections of how Set is a balanced force in the Egyptian pantheon. Set is the original spiritual rebel who indulges his true nature

---

[1] Private correspondence between Charles M. Pace and Cecil Williamson, 30 June, 1963.

within the mastery of darkness, storms, war and magick while also being a member of the Ennead and a protective (at times a syncretic) Neter (God). A Sethian or Luciferian may choose to gain experience and understanding (which leads to power, insight and results) to balance workings invoking Set with other (sometimes "enemy") Neteru who are used to harmonize his power for a purpose. Set is united at times with Horus, and Set protects the boat of Ra, mastering chaos in the form of Apep. Set is also a great magician. In some lore he is the father of Anubis and a lord of the desert. Amon-Ra, Isis, Sobek, Horus, Thoth and even Osiris can be approached from a Sethanic or Luciferian point of view.

It was Set who by his storming dark violence and rebellion against Osiris allowed the resurrected God of the Afterlife and Underworld (by way of the initiatory pain and struggle of physical death) to attain a much greater sphere and title of power by his necromantic resurrection by the Magician-Goddess Isis. Set introduced not only disruption, but also the destructive force which allowed the Xeper of Osiris to cross the abyss and ascend in his Apotheosis. This first negative and destructive act, bringing trauma and shock following the physical dismemberment of Osiris, motivated the greater deification and office of the gods to be assumed by Osiris. Motivation and the willed act of striving to overcome hardships and pain is a pure act of Magick.

Set is one of the most ancient of the Neteru, from the Naqada I Period dating to 4000-3500 BCE. Set appears among symbols carved on a mace head of a ruler known as Scorpion. In the Old Period, he appears in many Pyramid Texts, and in the Middle Kingdom Set is assimilated into the solar cycle of cosmology and theology as the strong Neter who, standing at the bow of Ra's ship, fought off and subdued the chaos serpent Apep (Apophis). The Heliopolitan Ennead identifies Set as being the son of Nut, the sky goddess, and the brother of Osiris, Isis and Nephthys. During the Hyksos Period, Canaanite tribes invaded and conquered much of the kingdom of Egypt. Their patron god was Baal (the storm god), who by syncretism and natural similarities of traits, was identified with Set.

After the downfall of the ruling Hyksos, the New Kingdom Pharaohs in the 19th and 20th Dynasties elevated Set to a major patron deity of the Ramessid kings (Sethos I - "Man of Seth;" Sethnakhte - "Seth is Mighty"), with Ramesses II having an arm of the royal Egyptian army named after "Seth." This royal family of the Ramessid rulers were from Avaris which had strong ties to Seth. Around the 25th Dynasty, Seth lost the veneration of the ruling cults and families of Egypt. Baal-Seth and Set-Typhon later survive and thrive as both war and storm gods, the most violent, however, as the demonic Typhon of the Greek myths.

Set possessed both great cunning and strength which he often applied to use. His epithet of "Great of Strength" refers to his scepter weighing a crushing 2,000 kg (or 4,500 lb)! Like the Syrian and Semitic "Azazel" and Tubal-Cain, Set is the Lord of Metals, including iron which was called the "Bones of Set." In balance, Set would assist the Ennead and the Order within the cosmos to equally bring chaos and disorder which threatened to destroy the cycle of nature and the rule of the Neteru.

Set was identified in part as a form of Apep (Apophis), while as a protective Neter he defends against this consuming darkness. Set's forms also include a human-headed deity of the ancient Canaanites known as Baal-Hadad, also as Baal-Seth fighting the sea god Yam (Leviathan) as well. Set could assume the form of creatures such as the donkey, antelope, pig, goat, crocodile, or hippopotamus, along with the animal-headed man as he was the most commonly depicted.

Coptic Magical traditions, assimilating Egyptian, Syrian, Greco-Roman and early Christian esotericism, revealed the many names and overall (mostly) beneficial protective spells of Set in a fluidic, chaos magical way, easily adapted by a resourceful Hermetic Magician or Sorcerer. As the Adversary, Set is the God of Chaos, Violence and War. One epithet, "The Red One" refers to his deification and rule over foreign lands, specifically the desert or "Red Land." Set inspires rebellion and strife, which for the Luciferian may be recognized as an unpleasant but powerful tool of motivation and Apotheosis depending on your alignment.

HEKA, THE BA, AND KA

Luciferianism has a specific tradition which explores the Egyptian pantheon from a Sethanic perspective. The magical traditions and methods of the Egyptians are great fountains of knowledge which unite the many inner-traditions and methods within history. This is an exciting perspective for the tools and knowledge available to the Luciferian. It is, however, too easy to get lost in the confusing esoteric concepts which can hinder the practice of Magick. To clarify what is the most important, I will define some key concepts and how they are utilized in practice.

Heka (Magick) is written in hieroglyphics in this form:

Heka (in Coptic transliteration "Hekau") is the Egyptian deification of Magick as a creative force, existing uniquely within the gods and connecting this power with not only nature, but also with the cosmic order manifest as the Ennead. Heka is, in simplicity, identified in two specific types or aspects: Heka the Neter and Heka the concept. The two are so deeply intertwined in Egyptian texts that the Black Adept can approach this power as either a Neter or type of power that emanates in currents. Heka is identified as the inherent power connected with the concept of the Ka (the spiritual double, the vital essence) of the sun god Ra (Re).

In Sethanic and Luciferian Magick, the Black Flame is a sometimes-interchangeable concept between the Ba, Ka and in a reflective sense, the Ren (name spoken to maintain its existence) to a more obscure point. The Ka is closely related to the Daemon, enhanced with Heka and Sekhem over time and experience. The Black Flame is essentially Heka as it is infused with the Ba and Ka of the Black Adept.

Heka is the enhancing and strengthening encircling force of energy assuming salient features of whatever deity the Black Adept embodies. Heka in the creations of Re-Atum appears and manifests before the emanation of Hu (utterance, creative word or the Gnostic concept of "Logos"). By authoritative utterance, described in myth as the act of practicing Sethanic Magick (or any other within and beyond Luciferian and LHP spectrums), the magician or sorcerer focuses Will, Desire and Belief to visualize each spoken word in the invocation, hymn or spell enhancing the Magickal vitality. This is the antinomian act of Left-Hand Path practice: you come into Being (like Khepri or the Setian concept of Xeper), enhancing your consciousness and performing and uttering Words of Power, which, like a god or goddess, either create or destroy. This involves self-accountability and the responsibility to our deified forebears, whose gift of the Black Flame opened our eyes in evolution. Magick or Heka is described by Ra (Re) to be his Ba or external manifestation.

In the Papyrus BM 10188, the god utters: "Magic is my Ka." In the Coffin Texts Spell 648, Heka declares his epithet, "Lord of Kas," referring to the myriad of ka-spirits within Heka's mouth. This directly connects to the concept of Words of Power. Uttering spells and hymns is an act of creative or destructive Magick and Sorcery. Heka's succession of forbidden knowledge is recognized in the effective authority and mastery the Neter possesses. With the utterance of a word, Magick penetrates and invests the Ka (vital essence) with either creative or destructive power.

For modern Sethanic and Luciferian Magicians inspired by the Egyptians, Heka ("magick") is a divine force that exists in the universe like "power" or "strength" and which can be personified in the form of the god Heka and even as the infusing power which enhances the Ka. The formula of Ankh-Ka-Djed-Ankh is the act of striving for balance and stability as you experience Liberation, Illumination and Apotheosis within the Grade Structure of the Sethanic Cult of Masks.

THE BA
Manifest Power which Illuminates and Enhances an Individual

The Ba is a representation of a deity or man in the entirety of physical and spiritual/psychic capacities and traits. Consider how you view yourself at your best and recent understanding, what you are "known" to represent: strengths, virtues and character. This, in a very simple basis, manifests power. The Ba is even a greater power among the gods and is the manifestation of power. The more powerful the god, the greater his Ba. The Black Flame is directly and abstractly associated with the Ba and Ka as well. The Ba is sometimes identified with perhaps part of the epithet, representing a manifestation of a god in which it is in a state in which it is manifest. The Neter Osiris is called the "living, golden Ba."

A cult epithet of Amun was "Horus, five living Bas which dwelt in Nun." The Ba may be perceived as the foundation animating spirit or essence based on mental (genetic and other) attributes which manifest in the way of character traits. The Ba is the aspect in which a Deific Mask or Neter becomes manifest within them.

The Ba is depicted with this hieroglyph:

The Ba visits the deceased body after death and is a principle element in the life of a man or woman. The Neteru also manifested in sacred animals such as the Ram of Mendes (called the "Ba of Osiris and the Bas of all gods manifest in all serpents"), who became identified with Baphomet. Amun is known from an epithet, "(Amun) august Ba of the Kematef-serpent." In the tenth hour of the Duat, a falcon is depicted resting upon a serpent in the Book of Amduat. It is known by the epithet, "Ba of Sokar-before-the-Duat." In a funerary text from the 12th Dynasty an interesting spell is recorded: "I am the great one whose name is not known; three rams are my Ba, six Khnums are my Shadow."

In the Pyramid Texts, the Ba was defined as a manifestation of specific power of a deceased king or Neter (God) in a state of which the power is manifest. Later, the Ba was a power of the living, dead, or gods manifest in the form it symbolized. Seth is the Neter which is inherent within storms, darkness and war. Thus, Seth is manifest in the energy that creates a response appropriate to the experience of natural effects on the physical world. This is the basis and most simplistic path of understanding of the Ennead and the Neteru of the Egyptian pantheon.

THE KA
Soul or Double

The Ka is understood as the "soul" and "double" of the individual. The Ka dwelt in the statue of man just as the Ka of a god could inhabit the statue of a god. This draws an association to accumulated energy which may be built into the idol or symbol of the specific Neter. The Sekhem (vital-energy including raw primal impulses) empowering the statue would not hold an independent "thinking" Neter, rather a subconscious link between the Black Adept and the God-form. A Black Adept who finds strong associations with a Neter would, by ritualistic identification with it and by directing and validating the energy enhanced by the Luciferian, honor both the Neter in question and the Daemon-Adept as well.

The Ka (Soul) is pictured with this hieroglyph:

The essence of the Ka was the soul which required nourishment after physical death in Egyptian religion. As offerings to the Ka would decrease, the Ka was then able to feed upon the offerings painted on the walls of the tomb, the images transforming into suitable energy for the Ka to absorb. This is very much in harmony with the concepts of

Astral Magick and nourishment of the essence of the psyche after death. The symbol of the Ka is the hieroglyph of two arms pointed upward. A devotional experience to the Neter by the Black Adept may lead to the careful ascension to the state of being known as a "Priest" of the Neter. Like Ptolemaic priesthoods of the Greco-Roman period, the office of priest, for example, with Alexander III of Macedon (The Great), would be limited to a specific time period. Some priesthoods were a lifelong journey, yet today the dedicated Magician can be so chosen by Set or other Neteru to hold the office of "Priest" for life. If you affirm a special "calling," learn all you are able to about that energy and Neter, applying it both in the spiritual and mundane world.

HEKA RISING BEFORE SET, THE UTTERANCE OF HU ILLUMINATES WITHIN THE BLACK ADEPT

Approaching these concepts within a pragmatic structure requires a clear understanding and perhaps even simplicity toward utilizing these concepts as a Luciferian and Sethian. Remember that a hymn, invocation or demonic incantation is an act of either symbolic or theological communication with deities or demons we associate with the abstract divine.

Adaptations in all my publications embody the grimoire with a distinct patron Spirit and are carefully created from ancient originals. Words and hymns name and command with the traits or epithets to encircle that type of energy or spirit to rise within you in this act of High Magick. When you utter an invocation, spell or hymn, remember that every single word you recite should be visualized in your imagination as actually happening at that very moment.

The Hermetic Circle or variants of Luciferian conceptions are different in purpose from the common and historical use of this defined boundary. Luciferians recognize and identify the magical circle as being a focused boundary to which you obsessively summon and invoke energy and the power associated with Deific Masks or other concepts in ritual. The Triple Hermetic Circle or others in our tradition are not to protect or keep out imagined or perceived spirits, powers or forces from you in ceremonial practice.

As a Luciferian, when you dedicate yourself by identifying with a power, you must make yourself confident and strong enough in mind and will to absorb, dissolve and change any energy which is negative to you. There is no other possibility acceptable except for this over-mastering and inherently Set-like act. The circle is a tool of encircling and focusing energy to further your goals.

HOW DO YOU VALIDATE AND RECOGNIZE THE MAGICAL EXPERIENCE?

If you can only describe it as an abstract and vague mass of "feelings" and "emotions," then trying to summarize it with "I felt this power or presence," then chances are you are spinning your wheels. Further, your actual performance of ritual is not invested to the point of exhaustion with Will, Desire and Belief.

There should be a build-up and increase of energy during the opening to middle stages of the ritual. Invoke with obsession and slowly build the chants and power to a climax in which the energy is released and directed with a total unity of Will, Desire and Belief. You must see it happen at that moment and allow the feeling of satisfaction and knowing it has been attained. This is measured by the momentum of energy you direct in the coming period creating and spinning the cycle of Liberation, Illumination and Apotheosis.

Deific Masks (including gods and demons) do not "talk" or communicate in the way that lessens and places them within our cultural context. If you invest belief and accept experiences in which deities, spirits or demons make a connection known to you, most likely it will be in the form of mental flashes and instinctual impulses. Your Daemon is the mediator of sorts for this communion with powers. This way our own Apotheosis interprets and applies the information received. Often, after writing it down, years later the instinctual impulse or images via the imagination will make clear sense of what knowledge was passed to you.

Part 11. Casting the Hermetic Circle: Magick in Practice

THE BASIC HERMETIC SETHANIC MAGICK CIRCLE

Balance and discipline are the essence and foundation for casting the Hermetic Circle as presented here. There are more in-depth and elaborate techniques and teachings of the Triple Hermetic Circle of Hamar'at, yet this is the simplistic version. Recognize that the forms of balance in the Triads are equal, essential, and the very foundation of our Ceremonial Magick.

TRIAD OF LIGHT	TRIAD OF DARKNESS
Amun-Ra (Light) - - - - - - - - - - -	Seth-An (Darkness)
Osiris (Life) - - - - - - - - - - - - - - -	Anubis (Death)
Isis (Love) - - - - - - - - - - - - - - - -	Sekhmet (Hate)

A Luciferian working with the Triad of Light and Darkness will be able to understand the balance of the opposing factions. It is not the duality which is worked with, it is how one works with each faction which is how they are utilized. For instance, Seth-An is known in Egyptian lore as the Strongest of the Gods and is the motivating power within each of us. This power is represented as the Tcham-scepter bearing the head of Set.

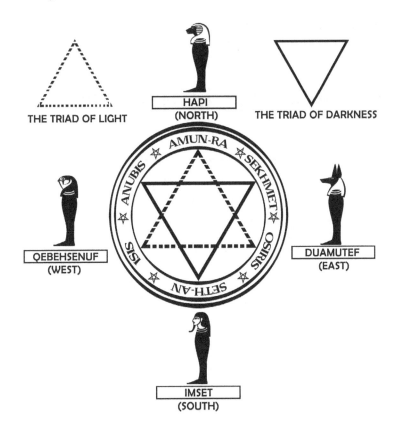

THE TRIAD OF LIGHT

HAPI
(NORTH)

THE TRIAD OF DARKNESS

QEBEHSENUF
(WEST)

DUAMUTEF
(EAST)

IMSET
(SOUTH)

While Set is Darkness, he also represents power and strength. When invoking Amun-Ra, Set is an empowering force with this Deific Mask. In the Stele of Anhotep, there is a Tablet of Set (numbered LXXVIII), which was made by a priest of Amun featuring a composite of Seth and Amun. The traditional Mask of Set, the night-hunting Seth-animal of the desert, wears the White and Red Crown unifying Upper and

Lower Egypt as well as a large standing statue showing the composite Deific Mask (Neter). In the Temple of Set in Ombos, there is a hieroglyph showing Amon and Seth sitting opposite, united. While you see that Set is a God of Darkness, storms and war he holds great power with other Neteru as well. This is the methodology of the Sethianist (or Luciferian, Setian, Typhonian Thelemite, Ceremonial Magician, etc.) of the approach toward Sethanic Hermetic Magick.

CASTING THE HERMETIC CIRCLE

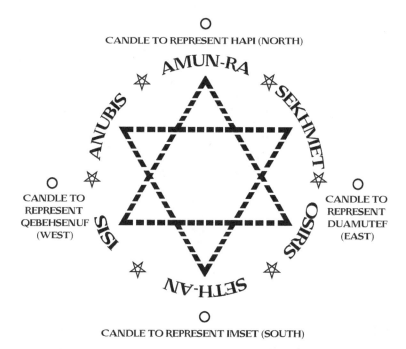

Ancient Egyptian above, English translation below. Prepare your altar space and the Hermetic Circle, candles, incense, sword (or athame), Tcham-scepter ("was-scepter" or wand), chalice, etc. You may utilize a large tapestry with the Hermetic design or simply place candles (white for the Triad of Light and black for the Triad of Darkness). Depending on desire, space and circumstances, over the years I have utilized my imagination as the sole ceremonial preparation (suggested only for experienced Black Adepts who have developed and grown comfortable with visualization), using a painted and drawn out circle, a printed tapestry of our design, candles marking the Triads, Canopic Jars marking the Four Sons of Horus (both small and large ones) and Neteru statues marking the cardinal directions. I have attained and validated short and long-term results from nearly every approach. Some may not be as fortunate. As a Neophyte, learn the art of casting the circle, the names and powers of the Neteru and the discipline to proceed with the spiritual intoxication and ecstasy of attaining gnosis with the union of Will, Desire, Belief made so by every word of the invocation.

Triad of Darkness

I. CALLING THE FOUR SONS OF HORUS

HAPI (NORTH)
Anet hra neter hen Hapi Ankh-Ka Djed-Ankh
Homage to thee, divine Hapi, soul-mate, everlasting life.

DUAMUTEF (EAST)
Anet hra neter hen Duamutef Ankh-Ka Djed-Ankh
Homage to thee, divine Duamutef, soul-mate, everlasting life.

IMSET (SOUTH)
Anet hra neter hen Imset Ankh-Ka Djed-Ankh
Homage to thee, divine Imset, soul-mate, everlasting life.

QEBEHSENUF (WEST)
Anet hra neter hen Qebehsenuf Ankh-Ka Djed-Ankh
Homage to thee, divine Qebehsenuf, soul-mate, everlasting life.

II. CLOSING THE ABOVE OR BELOW

With a sweep below and returning with a sweep above, you close both "as above so below" as this is the true casting of the circle and closing the circumference of self. If you are invoking a Neter of, for instance, the Ennead or a Deific Mask of the Triad of Light, the below closing would be appropriate. This creates a focused singularity of the type of energy and spirit you are to call within. If you are invoking a demonic or underworldly Neter, including workings of the Duat or the Chaos of Apep (Apophis), close the above to focus on the Triad of Darkness. Set, as you can consider, may be invoked from either the Triad of Light or Darkness, depending on purpose.

III. CALLING THE TRIAD OF LIGHT

With Invoking the Triad of Light, point your athame and move counter-clockwise focusing on the white candle. When invoking the Neteru, visualize and picture each while passionately calling forth the Deific Mask. The same is conducted with the Triad of Darkness.

FACE NORTH
Anet hra neter hen Amun-Ra Ankh-Ka Djed-Ankh
Homage to thee, divine Amun-Ra, soul-mate, everlasting life.

FACE SOUTH-EAST
Anet hra neter hen Asar Ankh-Ka Djed-Ankh
Homage to thee, divine Osiris, soul-mate, everlasting life.

FACE SOUTH-WEST
Anet hra neter hen Aset Ankh-Ka Djed-Ankh
Homage to thee, divine Isis, soul-mate, everlasting life.

IV. CALLING THE TRIAD OF DARKNESS

FACE SOUTH
Anet hra neter hen Seth-an Ankh-Ka Djed-Ankh
Homage to thee, divine Seth-An, soul-mate, everlasting life.

FACE NORTH-WEST
Anet hra neter hen Anpu Ankh-Ka Djed-Ankh
Homage to thee, divine Anubis, soul-mate, everlasting life.

FACE NORTH-EAST
Anet hra neter hen Sekhmet Ankh-Ka Djed-Ankh
Homage to thee, divine Sekhmet, soul-mate, everlasting life.

NOTE AFTER CASTING THE CIRCLE:

After the performance of the Triple Hermetic Circle invocation, the mind will be focused and directed toward the work of initiation and the accumulation of the divine within the temple of Mind-Body-Spirit. You may utilize a Hymn of Invocation to a Deific Mask based on your goal of the working.

V. INVOKING THE NETER

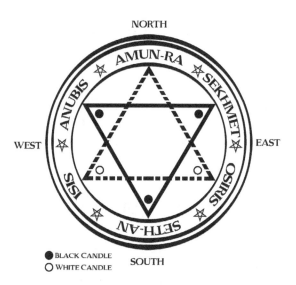

● BLACK CANDLE
○ WHITE CANDLE

Using incense and fumigation, invoke the chosen Neter utilizing the Hymns within "Necrominon" or a similar Egyptian text. As you gain experience in this ceremonial method, utilizing advanced techniques including the Triple Hermetic Circle is optional. The ritual of Ankh-Ka (Soul-Mate), High Luciferian Sex Magick, may be performed with your chosen partner once both of you are comfortable with the basic formula. Remember to use your imagination and trust your instincts. Magick is an Ancient Art which requires the Will, Desire and Belief of the Magician for it to impact your spiritual and mundane worlds. If you lack space and the proper privacy, adapt, and using the text, visualize and let your imagination be your ritual space. Close the ritual with repeating "So it is Done." Exit your chamber and feeling mentally and physically exhausted go indulge in some relaxation and cease all thoughts about the ceremony until you have rested.

RECOMMENDED READING

Kenneth Grant: Typhonian Trilogies 1-9, in chronological order: *The Magical Revival, Aleister Crowley and the Hidden God, Cults of the Shadow, Nightside of Eden, Outside the Circles of Time, Hecate's Fountain, Outer Gateways, Beyond the Mauve Zone, and Ninth Arch.* To be read along with it (It is apparent when to read it), read *Against the Light.*

Joan Ann Lansberry: *Images of Set*

Mogg Morgan: *Tankhem: Seth & Egyptian Magick, The Bull of Ombos, Supernatural Assault in Ancient Egypt,Phi-Neter: Power of the Egyptian Gods.*

Page, Judith, and Don Webb: *Set: The Outsider*

Judith Page & Ken Biles: *Invoking the Egyptian Gods*

Judith Page & Jan A. Malique: *Pathworking with the Egyptian Gods*

Webb, Don: *The Seven Faces of Darkness: Practical Typhonian Magic*

E.A. Wallis Budge: *The Gods of the Egyptians*

Temple of Ascending Flame

Temple of Ascending Flame is a platform for individuals around the world who want to share certain aspects of their work with the Draconian current with other adepts of the path and for those who simply need guidance into Draconian self-initiatory magic. It is both for newcomers who make their first steps on the Path of the Dragon and for experienced individuals who wish to progress on the Left Hand Path. We are not a "magical order." We do not charge fees for membership and our work is not based on any hierarchies. There are no restrictions on participation in our open projects, and in our inner work we welcome all who are capable of receiving and channeling the Gnosis of the Dragon.

More information: **ascendingflame.com**
Contact: **info@ascendingflame.com**

OTHER ANTHOLOGIES

RITES OF LUCIFER

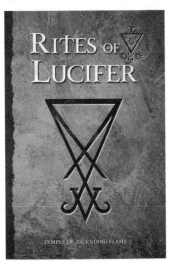

Lucifer is the archetype of the Adversary, initiator and guide on the Path of the Nightside. He is the fallen angel of Christian legends, the Devil of witches' Sabbats, one of primal Draconian Gods, Demon Prince of the Air, and Infernal Emperor of old grimoires. The purpose of this book is to delve into his initiatory role on the Draconian Path through chosen masks and manifestations which Lucifer has used over the ages to reveal his presence to mankind, bestowing his blessings on Initiates and scourging the ignorant. Essays and rituals included here explore both his bright and dark aspects, the face of the Light Bearer and the horned mask of the Devil.

Light and Darkness in Luciferian Gnosis by Asenath Mason - **The Light Bearer Ritual** by Temple of Ascending Flame - **Invocation of the Dark Initiator** by Temple of Ascending Flame - **The Mind of Lucifer** by Rev Bill Duvendack - **Purifying Fire (The Seed of Luciferian Gnosis)** by Edgar Kerval - **Lord of the Air** by Temple of Ascending Flame - **Lucifer - The Trickster** by Daemon Barzai - **The Shadow Companion** by Temple of Ascending Flame - **Holographic Luciferianism** by Rev Bill Duvendack - **The Adversarial Current of Lucifer** by Asenath Mason - **Invocation of the Adversary** by Temple of Ascending Flame - **Freedom through Death** by Cristian Velasco - **Emperor of Shadow and Light** by Pairika Eva Borowska - **The God of Witchcraft** by Temple of Ascending Flame - **The Infernal Spirit of Old Grimoires** by Temple of Ascending Flame - **Masks of Lucifer Ritual** by Rev Bill Duvendack

ISBN-10: 1505295092
ISBN-13: 978-1505295092

VISIONS OF THE NIGHTSIDE

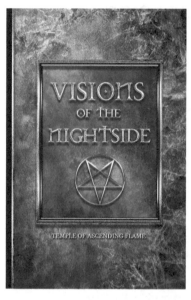

Collection of essays, rituals and various expressions of personal gnosis written by members and associates of the Temple of Ascending Flame. Unique and evocative in its content, the book comprises powerful manifestations of magical practice with the forces of the Nightside: dark gods and goddesses, primal energies of the Void, entities residing in the Qliphothic Tree of Death, demons of infernal regions, and spirits from a whole range of traditions. Compiled and edited by Asenath Mason, it is a practical research and insight into the magic of the Left Hand Path within the modern context, with contributions from working magicians and initiates of the Draconian Tradition.

Gnosis of the Void by Asenath Mason - **Setnacht** by Frater Eremor - **Hecate: Blessed Mother of Witches** by Pairika-Eva Borowska - **Mea Magna Mater Hecate. My Immersion in Multicolored Blackness** by Selene-Lilith - **Night on Bald Mountain: An Introduction to Slavic Witchcraft** by Febosfer - **Invocation to Lilith** by Asenath Mason - **Into the Void** by Frater GS - **Echoes** by Rev Bill Duvendack - **Ravens of Dispersion** by Asenath Mason - **Poseidon's Trident** by Rev Bill Duvendack - **Invocation of Sekhmet** by Asenath Mason - **The Lady of the Flame** by Asenath Mason - **Lucifer's Trident Ritual** by Rev Bill Duvendack - **Whispers From The Void (Exploration of Baratchial through the 12th Tunnel)** by Edgar Kerval - **Demeter: Draconian Goddess** by Fr. Nephilim

ISBN-10: 150865834X
ISBN-13: 978-1508658344

TREE OF QLIPHOTH

Tree of Qliphoth is our third anthology, exploring the dark side of the Qabalistic Tree as a map of Draconian Initiation. In essays, rituals and other expressions of personal research and experience, magicians and initiates of the Draconian Tradition discuss the realms of the Nightside, teachings and gnosis of its dark denizens, as well as practical methods developed both within the Temple and through their individual work. Material included in this book will give the reader a foretaste of these forces and a glimpse of what you can expect while embarking on the self-initiatory journey through the labyrinths of the Dark Tree.

Lilith by Temple of Ascending Flame - **In the Cave of Lilith** by Asenath Mason - **Naamah** by S.TZΣ. Swan - Gates of Naamah by M King - **The Dark Tower** by Calia van de Reyn - **Gamaliel** by Temple of Ascending Flame - **Lilith and Samael** by Asenath Mason & Rev Bill Duvendack - **Samael** by Temple of Ascending Flame - **Invocation of Adrammelech** by Rev Bill Duvendack - **Poisoned Well** by Rev Bill Duvendack - **A'arab Zaraq** by Temple of Ascending Flame - **Invocation of the Dark Venus** by Asenath Mason - **Invocation of Baal** by Rev Bill Duvendack - **Niantiel Working** by Asenath Mason - **Thagirion** by Temple of Ascending Flame - **Invocation of Belphegor** by Asenath Mason - **Invocation of Sorath** by Asenath Mason - **Thagirion** by Pairika-Eva Borowska - **The Cave of Lafcursiax** by Edgar Kerval - The **Qabalism of Lucifer's Sigil** by Rev Bill Duvendack - **Golachab** by Temple of Ascending Flame - **Invocation of Asmodeus** by Christiane Kliemannel - **Invocation of the King of the Nine Hells** by Rev Bill Duvendack - **Nine Hells of Asmodeus** by Asenath Mason - **Gha'agsheblah** by Temple of Ascending Flame - **Invocation of Astaroth** by Christiane Kliemannel - **Seven Gates of the Underworld** by Asenath Mason - **The Abyss** by Temple of Ascending Flame - **Invocation of Choronzon** by Rev Bill Duvendack - **Invocation of Shugal** by Rev Bill Duvendack - **Invocation of the Beast of the Abyss** by Rev Bill Duvendack - **Opening the Gates of Choronzon to Sitra Ahra** by Zeis Araújo - **Itzpapalotl** by N.A:O - **Ritual of Babalon** by Asenath Mason - **Satariel** by Temple of Ascending Flame - **Invocation of Lucifuge** by Christiane Kliemannel - **Summoning of the Lord of the Night** by Rev Bill Duvendack - **The Spider and the Web of Fates** by Asenath Mason & Pairika-Eva Borowska - **Ghagiel** by Temple of Ascending Flame - **Invocation of Beelzebub** by Christiane Kliemannel - **Litany to the Lord of the Flies** by Rev Bill Duvendack - **Experiencing the Strength of Belial** by Mafra Lunanigra-**Thaumiel** by Temple of Ascending Flame - **Invocation of Moloch** by Christiane Kliemannel - **Invocation of Satan** by Christiane Kliemannel - **Thaumiel: The Mask of Arrogance as Freedom** by Leonard Dewar - **The Calling of the Twin God** by Rev Bill Duvendack - **The Two-Headed Dragon of Thaumiel** by Leonard Dewar - **Invocation of the Lord of Thaumiel** by Rev Bill Duvendack - **Three Hidden Chakras Working** by Christiane Kliemannel

ISBN-10: 1530016320
ISBN-13: 978-1530016327

LILITH: DARK FEMININE ARCHETYPE

This anthology brings together essays, rituals, and unique artwork dedicated to the Queen of the Night and the Dark Goddess of the Qliphoth. Denied and rejected, worshipped and venerated, Lilith has been a part of the Western culture for ages. Viewed both as a beautiful seductress and a ruthless demon, she is the Serpent in the Garden of Eden, the first woman, and the primary initiatrix into the mysteries of the dark side of the Qabalistic Tree of Life. Her rites are the works of love and pain, sex and transgression, transcendence and immanence, for she exists at the roots of all desire of all humans past, present, and future. This archetype has never been fully grasped in its profundity and is constantly unfolding, challenging us to recognize our fears and passions and to transform them into tools of power. In this book you will find personal accounts of practitioners who ventured into the sacred and unholy garden of the Dark Queen of Sitra Ahra and returned transformed and empowered by her gnosis. Spells and invocations, dream magic and guided meditations, visions and stories of intimate encounters with Lilith - all this is contained in this unique anthology, written from the perspective of the Left Hand Path and the Draconian Tradition.

Asenath Mason: Introduction - **Mike King:** Sea of Ecstasy - **Kai'Nathera:** A Mother's Embrace - **Asenath Mason & Rev Bill Duvendack:** Fire and Lust - **Martha Gray:** Lilith and the Dual Nature of the Owl - **Nemo.V:** The Vase of Lilith - **Katie Anderson:** The Creative Fire: An Invocation to Lilith - **Edgar Kerval:** The Hidden Masks (A Lilith Exploration) - **Rev Bill Duvendack:** The Dark Feminine, a Man's Tale - **Asenath Mason:** The Unholy Grail - **Mike King:** Black Moon Lilith - **Selene-Lilith:** Selenic Face of Lilith - **Greg Brown (aka Ahohlan):** Journey into the Womb of Lilith - **Alisa Jones:** Lilith Queen of Tehiru Space - **Asenath Mason:** Lilith, Samael & Leviathan - **Leonard Dewar:** The Inconceivable Nature of Lilith - **Lucien von Wolfe:** Awakening the Vampire Within - **Rev Bill Duvendack:** The Mother of Abortions - **Asenath Mason:** The Mask of Medusa - **Rev Bill Duvendack:** Temple Astrological Correspondences

ISBN-10: 1979323267
ISBN-13: 978-1979323260